SUPERSTAR

SUPERSTAR

MANDY DAVIS

HARPER
An Imprint of HarperCollinsPublishers

Library of Congress Control Number: 2016939551
ISBN 978-0-06-237777-7

Typography by Carla Weise
17 18 19 20 21   PC/LSCH   10 9 8 7 6 5 4 3 2 1
❖
First Edition

For Ed

SUPERSTAR

The Meteor Shower

IT'S HARD TO SLEEP IN SHOES.

My feet are stiff. The pointy parts of the laces keep poking me. And every time I turn over, the sheets get all twisted around my legs.

But I can't take them off. Not now.

It's 1:58 a.m. In two minutes, Mom's alarm clock is going to beep, and when it does, nothing's going to slow me down, not even putting on shoes.

Last year, we saw nineteen superstars, and that was with a full moon, which makes them way harder to see. But the moon isn't out tonight and there aren't any clouds, which means we'll see more. I bet we'll see at least twenty-five.

Or thirty.

Or maybe even—

The beep. There it is!

I jump out of bed, grab the blanket by the door, and run outside to the middle of the yard away from the house and trees. When you're watching a meteor shower, you have to try to see as much of the sky as you can. You also have to be somewhere really dark. That's why our yard is perfect.

Our yard wasn't always perfect, though. When Dad was alive, we used to live in Florida in a town with a lot of streetlights that made it really hard to see the superstars. So every year, we'd drive out to Kennedy Space Center, where Dad worked, and watch them there. Sometimes the other astronauts would come too, and we'd all watch them together. Other times it was just Mom and Dad and me.

"Lester?" Mom yells. "It's pitch-black out here. Where are you?"

"Right where I always am."

She shines a flashlight across the yard.

"Turn it off! You're ruining the darkness."

"Lester, I'm not about to step in another molehill and twist my ankle again."

If she hurt her ankle, she'd have to go back inside and fix it up and then she wouldn't be out here with me and that would ruin everything.

Mom finally makes her way over to the blanket and flips off the flashlight. It's completely dark again.

We lie there for a while and wait.

And wait.

And wait.

I know what my dad used to say. *Wishing won't make superstars come any faster. The moment has to be just right.* But tonight everything seems to be taking so long. It feels like I'm never going to see any.

Just then, a bright light appears in the northeast, rockets across the sky, and disappears down by the horizon.

There it is! There it is! There it is!

"There's the first superstar of the night, Lester!" Mom grabs my hand and looks over at me, which means she's breaking the most important rule of superstar watching.

"Mom, you're supposed to keep your eyes on the sky the whole time, remember? If you don't, you might miss—"

But I stop talking because it's not possible to talk when the biggest and brightest superstar you've ever seen in your whole life appears in the middle of the sky. And then, another superstar, just as bright as the first, appears right next to it, and the two balls of light fall together toward the ground, leaving two streaks of light glowing behind them.

I keep my eyes focused on the spot where they were. I can still sort of see them there, like the light is burned into the sky.

We've seen a lot of superstars. Bright ones. Dim ones. Some are gone faster than you can blink. Others seem to hang in the sky. But we've never seen two at the same time before.

"A double superstar, Mom! And *we* just saw it!"

Mom sits up and stares at the ground in front of her.

"What are you doing?"

"Lester . . ."

"You're not even looking at the sky."

Mom reaches up and wipes tears out of her eyes.

She's crying? Why is she crying?

"Lester, I . . . I can't do this anymore."

"Do what?"

She stands up and runs toward the house.

"Mom?"

She can't leave now, not when we've only seen three super-stars and two of them were in the sky at the EXACT SAME TIME.

I'm standing now too, which means my eyes aren't on the sky anymore. They're on her. Running up the hill and onto the porch and opening the screen door.

"Mom!" I yell in my *emergency* voice.

She stops.

"Please don't go."

"Just keep counting, Lester. I'll be back in a little bit," she says, and runs inside.

She's coming back. Of course she's coming back. We've watched the Perseid meteor shower together every year of my life, every August for the past ten years. Even after Dad died and Mom and I moved to Indiana and stopped talking about Dad and space and what happened, we've never missed a meteor shower.

Ever.

I lie down on the blanket, stare up into the blackness, and wait.

A superstar shoots across the sky. That's number four.

And another. Five.

"Mom! You're missing them!" I yell at her.

I keep watching and waiting.

And counting.

Seventeen.

Eighteen.

Nineteen.

"Hurry up!" I yell toward the house. "We're almost to twenty."

I stare up into the blackness and wait for the screen door to squeak open.

But it doesn't.

The Morning After

WHEN I OPEN MY EYES, THE DARKNESS IS GONE AND THE SKY IS glowing. I'm still on the blanket.

All by myself.

Mom knows we always watch the superstars together. And she knows we only watch them once a year.

But that night's over, Mom wasn't out here for most of it, and now I can't even remember how many I saw. Was it twenty-six? Or twenty-eight?

When I get too tired, Mom's supposed to help me inside to bed and write down how many superstars we saw on a little notecard. Then, she's supposed to set it on my nightstand so it's the first thing I see when I wake up. But there's no notecard and I'm still outside and—

I pull my Superman action figure out of my pocket, squeeze my fingers around him, and rub my thumb over his red and yellow super *S*. Why didn't she come back out, Superman? Why?

She said she would.

She said to keep counting and she'd be back in a little bit.

I jump off the blanket and run toward the house. When I get inside, I'm going to walk straight into her bedroom and make her tell me why she never came back out.

But she's not in her bedroom. She's right there in the living room, asleep on the couch. The floor around her is covered with wadded-up tissues.

Seeing her like this . . . something moves in the way back part of my brain.

☆

It was five years ago, and we still lived in Florida. Mom was sitting on the couch folding towels. I was flying Superman around the living room. But Mom stopped folding and I stopped flying when the TV screen flashed from mission control to a video of bright blue sky with two balls of light and two trails streaking behind them.

The announcer's voice came on. *We are unsure exactly what happened at this time, but as you can see from this video, there are two trails of light instead of one. There are seven people on board.*

There were never two streaks of light before.

Mom dropped the towel she was folding.

"Why are there two, Mom? Which one is Dad's ship?"

She didn't answer.

The two streaks became three. Then four.

Mom turned off the TV and pulled me onto her lap. Then, we rocked. Tears dripped down her cheeks and onto my head. Her phone rang and rang and rang, and even though you're supposed to answer the phone when it rings, we didn't. We just stayed there and rocked.

After that, we spent lots of days going places where people patted my head and told me my dad was a hero. Mom spent lots of days lying on the couch, surrounded by tissues. Sometimes I'd lie with her. Other times, I'd fly Superman up into the sky, and use his superstrength to keep my dad's ship from breaking apart. Then, Superman and I would carry him back down to safety.

Over and over and over again.

The double superstar and those two streaks of light, it made her think of Dad. That's why she was crying last night and why I have to kick tissues out of the way to make a path to the couch.

I sit down next to Mom.

She rubs her eyes and looks around the room. "It's morning?"

"Yes."

"Oh, honey. I'm so sorry."

"It's okay," I say, because sometimes you have to say things you don't mean if you want to make your mom feel better.

"No, it's not. Lester, let me explain so you understand." Mom sits up and takes both of my hands in hers. "Those two superstars . . ."

"They looked like Dad's ship breaking apart."

Mom leans her head against mine. "It just felt like it was happening all over again." A tear drips down her face and lands on my arm.

I hand her a tissue.

She wipes her face with it, then crumples it up and throws it on the floor. "One more won't hurt, right?"

I know she's been doing this all night, but seeing her actually throw a dirty tissue on the floor—it's just so un-Mom-like that I start laughing.

She grabs another tissue and blows so long and loud it sounds like one of those horns the mountain men use to call their sheep. She crumples up the tissue and throws it backward over her shoulder.

Then I grab a tissue, hold it up to my own face, and do my best fake nose blow, which sounds more like a noise that usually comes out of the other end of my body. I wad up the tissue and toss it toward the TV.

Mom's laughing now, too. She takes another tissue. Blow. Toss.

I take another tissue. Pretend blow. Toss.

We keep blowing and tossing until the tissue box is empty and we're laughing so hard we can barely breathe.

When we finally stop laughing, Mom turns to me. "I could really go for some pancakes right now."

"You're going to make pancakes?" I ask. Mom never makes pancakes except on my birthday and sometimes on Christmas.

"Nah. I'm way too tired to cook. What do you say we go to the diner?"

"You mean the place where they pile up the pancakes in a big stack and put whipped cream on top?"

"That's the one." Mom puts her arms around me, but there's no time for hugs when giant stacks of chocolate chip pancakes with whipped cream are waiting!

Chocolate Chip Pancakes with Whipped Cream on Top

AFTER I FINISH MY GIANT STACK OF PANCAKES, I TRADE MY FORK for a spoon and scoop up all the syrup and whipped cream left on my plate. Forks work best for eating the pancakes themselves, but you have to use a spoon if you want to get every last bit of syrup. You can lick the plate too, which works best of all. I know because Mom actually let me try it once. But it took three showers to get all the syrup out of my hair.

Now, I just use a spoon.

"So, I take it you liked the pancakes," the waitress says, and picks up my empty plate.

"They're the best I've ever tasted!"

Mom looks across the booth at me. "Better than mine?"

"Uh-oh," the waitress says.

"You don't put whipped cream on yours, Mom. And sometimes your chocolate chips aren't melted. And that one time you burned them."

"He's right," Mom says. "Mine aren't nearly as good. Plus, food always tastes better when I don't have to cook it myself."

"Isn't that the truth." The waitress laughs and walks away.

That's when I get the idea. It's not a regular kind of idea like a plan for a new LEGO creation or even a great kind of idea like an idea for a new science experiment. This is a super, amazing, make-you-want-to-jump-up-and-down-if-your-Mom-says-yes kind of idea.

"Mom!"

"Yeah?" She takes another bite of pancake.

"We should come here and get pancakes every Tuesday."

"This was just a special thing we did today. We can't—"

"Sure, we can. Just listen to all the reasons. We already come into town on Tuesdays so we can do my lessons at the library instead of at home. The library is just down the street from here. I love pancakes. You love food you don't have to cook. Oh, and we could start calling Tuesday Pancake Day. It's perfect, Mom."

She reaches into her purse and pulls something out. "I have a surprise for you, Lester. Well, two surprises, really."

"You mean, presents?"

"Not exactly, but I think they're even better than Pancake Day."

Mom opens her hand. Inside is a blue plastic rectangle with words carved into the front of it. *Lucy Musselbaum. How may I help you?* There's a little white book icon next to her name.

"This is a library name tag, Mom."

"It is."

"And it has your name on it."

She smiles really big. "Lester, I got a job."

"At the library?"

She nods.

"The library we go to every Tuesday?"

She nods again.

If Mom works at the library, that means she'll be going there every day. And if Mom goes there every day, then I'll get to go there every day, too, because we always, always, always go to the library together. I'll sit at a work table and do my lessons and any time I have a question or need to look something up, it will be so easy because I'll be IN A LIBRARY!

"When do we start?"

Mom shakes her head no.

Why is she shaking her head no?

"Oh, Lester," she says, "you can't come with me."

"But we always go to the library together."

"I know we used to, but it's my job now and that changes things. I'll be cataloging books and helping people find what they need. I won't be able to be with you—"

"But I don't need you with me all the time, Mom. Remember last week? Remember how you said that since I'm ten now, I can spend time there by myself?"

"For an hour, Lester. Not six."

I pull my knees up into the booth and wrap my arms around them until I'm a tiny little ball. "But I can't stay home by myself. How would I make lunch? You said it's not safe for me to use the stove."

She grabs my hand. "You're right. It's not. That's why you're not staying home by yourself either."

I pull my hand away. "Mom, you're not making any sense! If I'm not going to the library and not staying home, what's going to happen to me?"

Mom smiles really big. "You get to go to school."

Away

OUR BOOTH STARTS TO DRAIN OF AIR. IT'S LIKE I'M IN A SPACE-ship's airlock chamber getting ready for a space walk, but I forgot to put on my oxygen tank.

"Oh, Lester, you're going to love it so much," Mom says. "You'll have science and math, just like we do at home. And a whole class for art. And you'll get to eat lunch in a cafeteria, and you'll have recess. And music class. Oh, and spelling. You're so good at spelling. And—"

She keeps saying more and more things about what school is like. The words pile on top of each other and fill up my brain and the booth and I know if I don't get out of here quick they're going to smother me.

So I run. Through the diner. Out the doors. Across the sidewalk. Onto the street.

Brakes screech. A car slides to a stop a few feet away from me.

But I have to keep running.

Past the carwash.

Past the grain silos.

Onto the railroad tracks.

"Lester!"

I keep going and going, stepping on railroad tie after railroad tie trying to outrun that word hanging in the middle of my brain.

School.

I don't *go* to school. I *have* school. With Mom. At the kitchen table. First, wake up. Then breakfast. Then math and reading. Then snack. Then writing. Then lunch. Then science and sometimes history, unless I can talk Mom out of it. That's how school has always been.

"Lester, stop!" Mom's right behind me. She grabs my arm and pulls me down off the train tracks to the edge of the cornfield. She's sucking in big gulps of air. "You almost. Got hit. By a car."

I pull Superman out of my pocket and straighten out his cape. If he stood in front of a speeding car, the car is the one that would die.

Mom puts her hand under my chin and raises my head up

so my eyes should be looking straight at hers, but I don't let them. I look at the ground, the corn, the sky.

"It's okay if you don't look at me," she says, "but I need you to listen."

I turn away from Mom and fly Superman in circles.

"Lester . . ."

"I'm listening!"

Even though I can't see her face, I can tell she's crying because of the snuffling sounds. "When I saw you run out in front of that car . . . Lester, you just have to be more careful. You . . ." She puts her hands on my shoulders. "Thinking about losing you . . . it just scares me so much."

"Well, I'm scared too!"

"About the car?"

"No." I sit down in the dirt. "About school."

Mom walks around and sits down facing me. "Tell me."

I don't mean to cry, but the tears just start pouring out. "It's just . . . I've never even been inside a school building before. I don't know what it will be like."

"Then we'll go there. You can see it before the first day, and then it won't feel scary anymore." Mom wipes the tears off my cheeks. "What else?"

"There are going to be other kids there."

"You'll make friends. You'll have someone else to talk to and play with." Mom takes Superman out of my hand and flies him around in front of me. "Doesn't that sound fun?"

I put Superman back in my pocket. "It sounds different."

Mom nods. "It is going to be different."

"And I'm going to have a teacher who isn't you."

"I bet your new teacher will be really nice. Maybe even nicer than me."

That makes me laugh. I can't imagine anyone being nicer than Mom. Or a better teacher. "I don't understand why you have to get a job."

She brushes the hair out of my eyes and behind my ear. "Lester, you know I love being your teacher. But I love other things too. Like books. And helping people."

"You never wanted to work at the library before."

"I used to be a librarian, Lester, and I loved it. But once you were born, I wanted to stay home with you more."

"And now you don't?"

"No, Lester, of course I want to stay home with you." Mom takes a deep breath. "There's another reason I need to get a job."

"What is it?"

"It's an adult reason, and you might not understand it."

"I might if you tell me."

So, she does. She tells me how expensive things are, like gas and food and having a house to live in. And she tells me how our savings is running low. If she doesn't get a job, we won't have enough money for the things we need. And even though I'm not an adult, I understand how important those things are.

"And getting a job is the only way?" I ask.

"It's the only way."

"Are you sure, Mom?"

"Lester . . ."

"What percent sure are you?"

"I'm one hundred percent sure."

That's the highest percentage there is. Which means I'm going to school.

Quarry Elementary School

QUARRY ELEMENTARY SCHOOL LOOKS A LOT LIKE QUARRY Library. It has the same red brick walls, the same metal slats on the windows, and the same rectangles of grass next to the sidewalk. But inside, I know it'll be much different.

"Come on, Lester. Once you know what it's like, it won't be scary anymore." Mom pulls open one of the doors and walks through. "Everything's going to be fine."

"How do you know?"

"I just do." She holds her hand out to me, but I don't take it. There's no way she could possibly know that everything's going to be fine.

"The sooner we go in, the sooner we can leave here and go to the library," she says.

That is true. And I do need to go to the library as soon as possible to work on my research.

I take a deep breath and follow her, first into a big open hallway and then into a room with a sign next to the door that says *Main Office*.

The lady sitting behind the desk looks up from her computer. "Can I help you?"

"I called a few days ago about enrolling my son, Lester Musselbaum."

The lady types something.

"We'd also like to tour the school," Mom says. "That way he'll know where to go on his first day."

"I won't be able to take you, but the school's open right now so you can go by yourselves." She types something else on her computer. "What was the name of his last school? I'll need to get his records sent over right away."

"Actually, we've been homeschooling until now."

The lady stares at me. Then she shuffles through a folder. "How old is he?"

"He just turned ten in July."

"That would make him a fifth grader. Let me check class sizes." She spins in her chair and clicks through a few screens on her computer. "That'll put him in . . . hold on." She clicks a few more times, then lets out a big breath. "Mrs. Raines's class. Room seventeen."

She grabs a map of the school, circles room 17, and

scoots it across the desk toward me. Then she hands Mom a clipboard with some papers on it. "Fill these out. You can sit over there."

Mom works on the papers while I study the map of the school. *Room 17—Raines*. It's right there between *room 16— Perez* and *room 18—Turner*. I follow the path from the main office to room 17 with my finger. It doesn't seem too hard. Just three turns.

A few minutes later, Mom takes the clipboard back up to the lady. "I'd like to speak with the principal, if I could."

The lady picks up her phone and pushes some buttons. "Mr. Marmel, yes. Mrs. Musselbaum would like to see you . . . uh-huh . . . uh-huh." She hangs up the phone. "You can go on in." She points to a door at the side of the room that says *Principal* in big, black letters across the glass.

I stand up.

"Lester, I need you to stay out here."

"By myself?"

She pulls her chair over close to mine. "Just for ten minutes or so. There's a clock right there on the wall. You can count down the minutes if you want to."

"You can't leave me alone with a stranger."

"She's not a stranger. Everyone who works at your school is a safe person."

Mom stands up and walks over to the *Principal* door.

"I'll be back soon and then we can take that tour of your new school."

I study the map for a while. The building is really just a big square with hallways coming off every corner. Pretty soon I know how to get from my classroom to every other room in the school.

"There's a box of Legos in the conference room if you want to go play with them." The lady behind the desk points down the hall.

"LEGO *bricks.*"

"What?"

"You have to call them LEGO *bricks,* not *Legos.*"

"And why is that?"

"Because of the rules. You're not supposed to put an *s* on the end of the word LEGO. You're supposed to put a noun after it, like LEGO *bricks* or LEGO *creation.* And you also have to capitalize all the letters in LEGO."

Her eyes move in a half-circle around the top of her eye sockets. "Fine. There's a box of capital-letter LEGO *bricks* in the conference room if you want to go play with them."

"Are they sorted by shape and by color?"

"No! It's just a big box of Legos."

"LEGO *bricks.*"

She opens her mouth like she's going to say something else, but closes it again when a really tall woman walks into the office from down the back hallway. The woman puts a paper in the slot on top of a big machine at the side of the room and pushes some buttons. When the machine starts whirring and whooshing, the woman turns and walks over to the desk.

"I'm sorry, Regina." The front desk lady puts a piece of paper up to her face so I can't see her mouth, but I can still hear her.

"For what?" the woman asks.

The lady points at me. "That's Lester Musselbaum. He's in your class."

That's her. That's my teacher. I look up at her face so I can memorize it.

"I don't remember a Musselbaum on my list."

"He just enrolled today."

"Well, now I'm up to twenty-eight."

"Twenty-eight what?" I ask.

"Where'd he move from?" She looks over at me then back at the other lady. "Don't tell me Greenville. They're always so far behind."

The front desk lady leans in. "He didn't move *from* anywhere. He was homeschooled."

"And you gave him to me?" my teacher whispers. "Mary, you know this is my last year. I've already paid my dues."

"I had to, Regina. Ana was already at twenty-nine, and you only had twenty-seven."

The machine stops. My teacher picks up the pile of papers

from the side. "*Only* twenty-seven." She puts one of them in the slot on top of the machine and pushes a button. The machine whirrs and whooshes, but this time, it stops after spitting out just one paper.

"Twenty-seven what?" My voice is louder now.

"Students." My teacher looks over at me. "And it's twenty-eight, including you."

Twenty-eight kids? In the same room? All the books I've read for my school research showed pictures of fifteen kids at most. I know because I counted them. But never twenty-eight. That's almost thirty, which is fifteen times two.

My teacher grabs the paper off the machine and adds it to her stack. "Welcome to school, Lester Musselbaum."

Research

WHEN WE GET TO THE LIBRARY, I GRAB THE LAST FIVE BOOKS off the "Back to School" bookshelf and head to my study table in the corner of the children's section.

"Almost done with that school research of yours?" Miss Jamie asks as I walk by her desk.

"I have to be almost done. School starts tomorrow."

Tomorrow.

I'll be in my new classroom. With my new teacher. And all those kids I've never met before.

"Did you know I used to live in Texas when I was a kid?" Miss Jamie asks.

I shake my head no.

"I loved it there, Lester. We had this big house on a street with giant trees and my best friend Maria's family lived two houses away. Every summer Maria and I would ride our bikes down to Mr. Alister's pond and swim and catch frogs. This one time, Lester, we decided we were going to keep one of those frogs as a pet, so we brought him home and put him in the bathtub." Miss Jamie laughs. "You should have heard my mom scream when she went to take a shower that night."

"Miss Jamie, I need to do my research now!"

"'Tis true, my dear." She holds a finger up in the air. "But you also need to hear this story. You see, this one day, those squirrely parents of mine up and decided we were moving to Indiana. I didn't want to go. I cried and begged and made deals, but a few months later, our house was packed in a yellow moving truck and all four of us kids were piled into the back of the station wagon. We drove right out of the Lone Star State and never looked back. Well, that's not exactly true. My sister and I looked back the whole way because we were sitting in a seat that faced backward—"

"Miss Jamie . . ."

"Yes, yes. I know we're burning daylight here. But the thing is, Lester, I met Paula in Indiana. And even though we never caught a frog, we got a rabbit once and kept it for two weeks before my mom found out. And Paula's still my friend, Lester, over thirty years later. Do you understand what I'm saying?"

"That you have a friend named Paula."

"No, Lester, I'm saying that maybe you'll meet *your* Paula

27

at school." She smiles at me.

In less than twenty-four hours I'm going to be at school, I don't have my research done, and I'm standing here listening to Miss Jamie tell me I might meet someone named Paula?

"I have to finish my research now," I tell her, and walk away before she can say anything else.

When I get to my study table, I open up the top book in my pile: *School, School, Here I Come*. There's a little cartoon mouse wearing a backpack on the front cover.

School, school, here I come.
Time for learning, time for fun.

I write *learning* and *fun* in my research notebook.

Time for staying in the lines
Time for reading—

The kid at the next table is staring down at a page of double-digit subtraction problems and talking to himself.

It's really hard to concentrate on reading when someone at the next table is saying math problems out loud. It's even harder to concentrate when he's doing them wrong.

"The answer's forty-seven," I tell him.

"What?" He looks up from his paper.

"You did it wrong." I explain the steps. That way he'll understand how I got the right answer.

He reaches over and grabs *School, School, Here I Come* out of my hand. "Yeah, well, you're reading a book for babies." He flips through the pages like he doesn't even care if he rips them. "This looks like something my little sister would read."

"It's for research."

"What are you researching? Mousies?" He moves the book around like the mouse on the front cover is dancing.

"The plural form of mouse is mice. And if I were researching mice, I wouldn't use a book with a cartoon on the front cover."

"Whatever, baby," he says, and throws the book back on the table.

I turn away from him and stare down at the page.

Time for staying in the lines.
Time for reading books with rhymes.

"What are the mousies doing now?" he asks.

"The *mice* are reading."

He leans back in his chair. "I hate to break it to you, baby, but mousies don't read."

"I know that mousies—"

He laughs.

"Mice! I meant to say mice!" I slam the book down on the table. "And I know that mice don't read, but in books, animals can do things they don't do in real life. Didn't you ever read *Charlotte's Web*? All the animals talk to each other in that book *and* it has an award sticker on the front, which means it's a very good book."

"Does your mousie book have an award sticker on it?"

I look at the front. Then the back. No stickers.

The kid laughs. "That's what I thought."

A man carrying a little girl walks up behind the kid and puts a hand on his shoulder. "You do remember you're supposed to turn that packet in to Mr. Jacobsen first thing tomorrow morning, right?" He sits down next to the kid. "Now let's look at this one. What's seven minus nine?"

The kid says *two* in a really low voice.

"I think you mean negative two," I say.

The man smiles at me. "We're not quite to negative numbers yet." He turns back to the kid. "Let's try it again."

The kid puts his head down on the table.

"Fine," the man says. "Samantha has her new book now. We can finish your packet at home."

As they're walking away, the little girl points to my book. "Look, that book has a mouse on it too!" She holds up a book with a mouse and a flower on the cover.

"Ha! I told you that book was for babies," the kid says to me. He grabs his packet off the table and follows the man. That's when I notice his shoes. Bright red. White laces. Tall enough to cover his ankles. I didn't even know they made shoes like that. My shoes are always white and short and boring.

"See you later, Mouse Boy," the kid says, then turns the corner and walks out of the library.

I stand up to scream at him, to tell him to stop calling me baby and Mouse Boy, but my chair crashes to the floor and everyone in the children's section stares at me.

All six of them.

And so many eyes on me all at once hurts my stomach. So does being called something that is not my name.

Is that what it's going to be like tomorrow? Are the kids in my class going to be mean to me?

None of the books said anything about mean kids. They all talked about being a good friend and how to be nice to each other. One book even said that being nice to people is a school rule. And a rule is something you have to follow.

But I'm not at school yet. I'm at the library and there's not a being-nice rule here, just a being-quiet rule.

Tomorrow at school, everything will be different. That's what it says in my research, and what you learn in research is always true.

First Day of School

WE PULL INTO THE SCHOOL PARKING LOT AND FIND A PARK-ing spot.

"You're going to be fine," Mom says for about the millionth time. She said it when we were here last week and almost every evening at dinner and last night when she tucked me in to bed. She says it every time we're talking about school and even sometimes when we're not.

I check the clock on the dash—8:56. School starts at nine o'clock, which means we only have four minutes left to get to my classroom. I can't be late. Being on time is a rule.

Mom and I hurry through the parking lot and up the sidewalk and through the double glass doors. I keep one hand in my pocket, holding on to Superman. Just in case.

The hallways are mostly empty, and after a few turns, we're standing in front of a large wooden door with the name *Raines* next to it.

I look through the little slit of a window. Kids are everywhere. Putting stuff in desks. Hanging up backpacks. Walking around. Talking. I try to count them to see if there really are twenty-seven, but they keep moving.

Mom opens the door right as a bell dings. We step inside and stand in a big open area in the back of the room. There are desks in rows, facing away from me. In the far corner is one really big desk with a computer on it. Across the room from us, there are two large windows. At the back of the room is a closet with hooks where kids were hanging their backpacks.

The kids all sit down at their desks, which makes it much easier to count them. There are four rows, with seven desks in each row, but two of the desks are empty. Counting me, there are twenty-seven kids in here right now.

Someone must be missing.

A low voice booms from a speaker in the ceiling. "Good morning, Quarry Elementary students. Welcome to another wonderful year. For all you new kindergartners, I'm your principal, Mr. Marmel. Today is a real beginning for you. Not only the beginning of your six years here at Quarry, but the beginning of your whole schooling career. And fifth graders . . ."

The kids in my room cheer.

"Today is the beginning of the end. Your last year here

at Quarry Elementary. Let's make it your best year yet!" The speaker crackles off, and the room is quiet.

My teacher is standing in front of the room, leaning on a tall rectangular thing that looks like a little desk with an angled top. She's looking at me. The kids are looking at me.

I step behind Mom. Even though I have pages of school research in the notebook in my bag, I don't know anything about this place. I don't know this teacher or these kids. I don't even know where to sit. "Don't leave me here, Mom."

"Remember all those things we talked about?" Mom whispers. "All the things you're going to learn? All the different classes?"

"We're waiting," my teacher says.

"Where would you like him to sit?" Mom asks.

"Oh, that back seat over there will be fine." She points a long wooden stick at the far row.

Mom turns back to me. "I'll be out front at three o'clock to pick you up."

"Please don't go!" I look up at her, eye to eye, to show her how serious I am.

"You're going to be fine."

There it is again. That thing she keeps saying. And I want to believe her. I want it to be true. But right now it feels like the biggest lie ever.

Mom squeezes my hand and walks out the door. She

waves the I-love-you sign at me through the window. Then she's gone.

I shove my hand in my pocket and squeeze Superman as hard as I can.

My teacher makes a noise like she's got something stuck in her throat. "What do you think, Lester Musselbaum? Are you planning on sitting down? Or are you waiting for a formal invitation?"

A few of the kids laugh. Why are they laughing? No one told a joke.

"While Lester is finding his seat, I'll start the introductions. I'm Mrs. Raines, although you probably already knew that. But what you might not know is that we all have something in common. Mr. Marmel mentioned that this is your last year here at Quarry. Well, it's my last year here, too. I've been teaching fifth grade in this same room for the last thirty-nine years. And one year from today, I'll be . . . well, let's just say that I won't be here anymore."

The classroom door swings open.

Please be Mom. Please be Mom.

But it's not. It's a kid. A little taller than me with yellow spiky hair. I feel like I've seen him somewhere before, but I can't figure out where until I see his shoes. Those bright red shoes.

I tiptoe backward.

"Ricky," Mrs. Raines says, "I was wondering if you'd be gracing us with your presence today."

Ricky. That's what the man called him yesterday in the library.

"Would you care to share what sort of emergency caused you to be late on the very first day of school?" Mrs. Raines asks.

Ricky doesn't say anything. The whole room is quiet. And the kids aren't staring at me anymore. They're staring at him.

"Maybe you'll remember later. Say, around recess time? But for now, let's find you a seat. I can start the year with one kid standing in the back of the room, but not two."

Ricky turns around. "Mouse Boy? I didn't know they let babies into the fifth grade."

Words bubble up from my chest and explode out of my mouth. "MY NAME IS LESTER AND I'M NOT A BABY!" Twenty-eight pairs of eyes burn into me like laser beams.

I run out into the hallway, pull Superman out of my pocket, and fly him around and around and around.

Who are we going to save today, Superman? I try to think of someone, but right now, there's only one person who needs saving.

Me.

Mrs. Raines walks out the door. "Lester, I have no idea why—" She grabs Superman out of my hand. "You're out here playing?"

"No."

"Lester, I saw you." She wraps her long bony fingers around Superman until all I can see is the top of his head and the tips of his boots. "I'm holding the toy you were playing with."

"At home—"

She bends down so we're face-to-face. "Do you see a bed here, Lester?"

A bed?

"Or a couch?"

There's nothing in the hallway except doors and a drinking fountain.

"What about a stove? Do you see someone frying bacon over there?" She points to a section of hallway that's completely empty. "If you haven't noticed yet, Lester, this is not your house. You're at school now. And we don't play with toys during the school day."

"I wasn't playing with him."

She crosses her arms. "Do you know what I usually do when I find a student playing with a toy?"

Of course I don't know. I don't know anything about this place.

"I put that toy in a drawer and it doesn't come out again until the end of the year."

A year? I can't lose Superman for a whole year.

"When you return to the classroom, you will go to your seat and follow all of my directions. If we have any more trouble, Superman goes into the drawer."

But there will be trouble. I know there will. There were only two empty desks, which means I'm going to have to sit by that Ricky kid and he's probably going to call me baby and Mouse Boy. Then I'll get mad again and Mrs. Raines will put Superman in the drawer.

"Come on," Mrs. Raines says.

"I can't sit by him," I tell her.

"I know," she says, and walks back into the room.

I peek around the corner. There's a girl sitting in front of my empty desk. A girl with long black hair. I look at her and she smiles at me, just like the kids in my school research books.

Ricky's all the way on the other side of the room, hunched over his desk putting books away. The girl is still smiling at me.

I walk into the classroom and sit down.

"Hi," she says. "I'm Abby."

"I'm Lester," I tell her.

"I know," she says, and looks down. "You sort of yelled it earlier."

The yelling. I forgot about that.

"Lester is a very old-fashioned name, but I like it. Names are like clothes, you know. If you wait long enough, they always come back into style." She leans over my desk toward me. "Ricky has been in my class every year since third grade."

"Has he always been so mean?" I ask.

She nods yes. "And he's not the only one. See that kid up in the front of our row?"

I lean out into the aisle to get a better look. He's way bigger than me and has on the kind of shirt that looks like he should be out on a field playing some kind of sports.

"That's Connor," Abby says. "He's Ricky's best friend. If you think Ricky's bad on his own, you should see them together."

Ricky is suddenly looking right at me, and our eyes meet for a split second. I turn back to Abby.

"But you have to be nice to people in school. That's a rule, right?"

She leans in even closer. "I guess it's a rule. But they're sneaky, Lester. If the teachers don't find out, they always get away with it." She grabs a folder out of her desk. "Anyway, enough about that. I have something for you."

She opens the folder and pulls out a little card. It's sparkly pink on one side and on the other side, it says: *Abby Chin, Fashion Designer Extraordinaire* and has an email address and a phone number on it. "It's not my number, by the way. It's my mom's. But she lets me use her phone whenever I want." Abby holds her hand out to me. "It's very nice to meet you, Lester."

I shake her hand. "It's very nice to meet you too, Abby."

"And if you ever need any designing work done," she says, "I hope you'll consider me for the job."

Abby turns around and starts arranging the books in her desk.

Even though I'm not exactly sure what a fashion designer is or why I would need one, I have a feeling this card is something I should keep safe. I slide it in my pocket where Superman usually goes.

Hungry

SUPERMAN SITS ON MRS. RAINES'S DESK ALL MORNING. HE'S ON her desk for spelling and reading and writing. He's on her desk when I get really hungry and raise my hand to ask when snack is. He's on her desk when Mrs. Raines says that fifth graders don't get snack and I ask what fifth graders get and she walks over to the schedule on the whiteboard and points to the word *lunch* and everyone laughs.

At home I got snack. In some of my school research books the kids got snack, too. But here you don't. At this school, you have to go all morning with nothing to eat since breakfast and it feels like your stomach is so hungry it's trying to eat itself.

But you can't argue and say you need something to eat right now because that would be making trouble. And if you make

41

trouble, your teacher will put your Superman in the drawer where he won't come out again until the end of the year.

So I listen to Mrs. Raines talk about compound sentences, and I do my English worksheet and turn it in to the tray. Then I sit back down and wait.

When it's finally time for lunch, the class walks to the cafeteria in something Mrs. Raines calls a single-file line, which means everyone walks right behind the person in front of them. At the corner, our line splits. Some kids go straight into the big cafeteria room. Others keep walking down the hallway. I have to eat as soon as possible so I follow Abby toward the cafeteria door.

"Where's your lunch?" Abby asks.

"I'm getting spaghetti."

"Then you have to go through the kitchen line." Abby points at the long line down the hallway in front of us. "That's where you get your food. You can only come in here if you brought your lunch."

So I walk down to the spaghetti line and stand at the very end.

Stupid long line.

Stupid late lunch.

Stupid school.

When I finally get to the kitchen door, I can see why it's been taking so long. There's only one lady serving food. One lady for all these kids?

"I suppose you'd like some spaghetti too," she says when I get up to her.

"Yes, I want spaghetti! That's why I've been standing in this stupid long line."

She puts down her giant spoon and crosses her arms.

"What are you doing? You're supposed to be getting me food like you did for all the other kids."

"The other kids didn't call my line stupid."

"It's just . . . I think you should have two people serving food. Or maybe even three. Then everyone would get their food way faster."

The lady stares at me.

"Please! I'm so hungry."

She picks up the spoon and piles a heap of spaghetti in the big rectangle part of my tray. Then she scoops a bunch of pears into the circle area and puts a piece of garlic bread in the square. "Blame the budget cuts, kid. Not me," she says, and scoots the tray across the metal counter.

I don't even care what budget cuts are. There's food on this tray and it's mine. All mine. I pick up the garlic bread to take a bite.

"Drop it!" she yells, and points to the wall behind me.

There's a big sign that says: *No Eating in the Kitchen*.

"Get on out to your table. I need to start cleaning up."

I grab my tray and walk toward the door, but as soon as I step out into the cafeteria, I have to come right back inside.

"I thought I told you to go on out there," the lady says.

"I can't. It's too loud."

"You've got that right. Every time I have table duty, I go home with my ears ringing. Now go find a seat."

I keep my back pressed against the door.

She walks over to me, grabs the door handle, and starts pushing it closed.

"No! Stop!"

But she doesn't stop.

"Please! I can't stand it out here!" I yell, but she probably can't hear me because *I* can't even hear me.

She pushes the door closed. Now I'm all the way out.

The sound fills my head like a tornado, swirling and swirling and if I don't do something quick to stop it, I know my head is actually going to explode. I push backward against the door but it's completely closed now. There's nowhere to go. I can't think. I can't think. I can't think with all this noise in my head! I have to make it stop and the only way to do that is to stick my fingers in my ears.

Everything turns quiet.

My tray falls to the floor like it's moving in slow motion. Spaghetti sauce and pears splatter across the tiles. The garlic bread slides over to the table of kids closest to me. They look at me. Then the next table looks at me. Then the next table. In a few seconds, the whole cafeteria is staring at me.

I try to turn the handle of the door behind me, but it's locked. The only thing I can do is run.

Past the tables.

Out the door.

Down a hallway.

Down another hallway. I'm going too fast; they all look the same.

I finally stop when I get to two wooden doors I've never seen before. A bright light in the ceiling shines down on them. The sign on the wall says *Library* in big black letters.

There's a library here? In my school?

It's like the real library only smaller. Rows and rows of bookcases fill the room. And no one's here. It's absolutely, perfectly quiet. I walk along the rows of shelves, running my fingers along the spines of the books. Picture books. Chapter books. Reference books. Novels. And the nonfiction section!

Five huge nonfiction bookcases line the back wall of the library. I squeeze into a little space between two of the book-cases. The wood and all the books on the shelves hold me there, nice and tight and safe. This is definitely my favorite spot in the whole school. Or maybe the whole world. The only part of me that doesn't want to close my eyes and stay here forever is my stomach.

The food was right there in my hands. The warm noodles. The meaty sauce. The chewy, buttery garlic bread. Except for when I sleep at night, this is the longest I've ever gone without food.

But now my lunch is spread across the cafeteria floor, and I'm in a library. I know there's no food in here because food isn't allowed in libraries. It could ruin the books.

I lean my head on my knees, and that's when I notice the glob of meat sauce on my shoe. There *is* food in here! I touch my finger to the top of the sauce and taste it. Tomatoey. Beefy. It doesn't taste like old, dirty shoe at all. And it's still warm.

So I scoop the rest of it up and eat it. I check my other shoe and my socks and legs, but there aren't any more splatters of sauce anywhere.

The lady from the front office walks around the bookcase in front of me. "Did you just eat something off your shoe?"

"I didn't have any books out. Nothing got ruined."

She stares at me for a second. "Well, come on. We're going to the office."

"Is there food there?"

"No."

"Then I'll just stay here."

"You most certainly will not stay here." Her voice is louder now. "You will be paying a visit to Mr. Marmel, and he's probably going to call your mom."

"Really?" I look up at her.

She smiles a little.

I smile a little, too. "Do you think he'll call her right away?"

"Maybe. This is a pretty serious situation you've gotten yourself into."

I push myself out from between the bookshelves and follow the lady to the office. Of course it's a serious situation. Except for the sauce on my shoe, I haven't eaten in over five hours.

Mr. Marmel

WHEN I GET TO MR. MARMEL'S OFFICE, HE'S SITTING BEHIND A big wooden desk.

"Can you call my mom now?" I ask him right away.

"Lester, sit down." Mr. Marmel's voice is much softer than it was this morning on the loudspeaker.

"Are you going to call her then?"

He doesn't say anything. He just points to the wooden chair in front of his desk.

I don't know if that means yes or no, but I sit down anyway, just in case it means yes.

"Why are you in my office right now, Lester?"

"Because that lady brought me in here."

He shakes his head. "I know you're new to our school, and

48

I'm trying to be patient, but I need some cooperation here, Lester." He interlocks his fingers and sets his hands on the yellow notepad on his desk. "Now. Tell me why you're here."

I try to think back in case there's something I missed. I was sitting in the library. The lady came and got me. If it wasn't for her, I'd still be in the library.

"Well?" Mr. Marmel crosses his arms. "I don't like having to answer my own questions, Lester."

He's wearing a suit and tie and has gray old-person hair and rectangular glasses. He looks like someone who should be smart, someone who might go to the library and check out books, maybe even books about space. But right now he's not making any sense.

"If you already know the answers, why are you asking me?"

"Are you trying to get yourself in trouble?"

"No, I'm—" Trouble? *If we have any more trouble, Superman goes into the drawer.* "I'm not trying to get in trouble! Please don't tell Mrs. Raines I am. Please!"

"Then the next words out of your mouth better be an answer to my question."

But I don't know the answer. I pull my knees up to my chest, wrap my arms around them, and rock myself back and forth.

It doesn't help. Not way up here on this chair and out in the open. Rocking only helps if you're somewhere cozy and dark. I slide down off my chair and sit just underneath the edge of Mr. Marmel's desk. My stomach growls again.

Back and forth. Back and forth.

Food.

Superman.

Food.

Superman.

"What on earth are you doing now?"

He's not supposed to talk to me when I'm rocking. He's supposed to leave me alone, like Mom does when I sit on the floor at the foot of my bed and rock until I can think straight again.

Back and forth. Back and forth.

Food.

Superman.

Food.

Food.

Food.

"If you aren't going to cooperate," he says, "I'm going to have to call your mom."

"Yes!" I jump out from under his desk. "Call her! And tell her to bring me some food. Tell her I haven't eaten in over five hours and that I've never gone that long without eating. Tell her that I'm sorry about dropping my tray but my head felt like it was going to explode from all that noise. The cafeteria lady closed the door behind me and I couldn't think of what else to do to make the noise stop so I put my fingers in my ears and my tray crashed to the floor. I know fifth graders don't get snack but I didn't get to eat lunch so just tell her to bring me something to eat!"

"Lester—"

"Here." I pick up the phone and hold it out to him. "I know she'll come."

He takes the phone and presses a button. "Mary, will you please go down to the cafeteria and get a tray of food before it's all put away?" He hangs up the phone.

"You didn't call my mom."

"Mrs. Caldwell is getting a tray from the cafeteria."

"For me?"

"Yes. Now go sit over there." He points to a table by the window. "Your food will be here in a minute."

One minute! In only one minute, I'll finally have my spaghetti and garlic bread!

It ends up taking longer than a minute. It takes two minutes and forty-seven seconds, to be exact, but when the door swings open and the front desk lady walks in with a tray of food, I don't even care.

"Try not to drop this one," she says, and sets the tray on the table.

I grab a fork with one hand and my tray with the other. The only place this food is going is in my stomach.

Math Test

WHEN I GET DONE EATING AND GO BACK TO MY CLASSROOM, I walk straight over to Mrs. Raines's desk and check on Superman. He's right where he's been all morning.

"I still get him back at the end of the day, right?"

Mrs. Raines puts her finger up to her lips and points behind me. The kids are all working at their desks. The only sound in the room is pencils writing.

Mrs. Raines hands me a packet. "Here. It's a math pretest to see what you already know."

"Superman's still on your desk and not in your drawer. That means I get him back, right?"

"Not if you don't start working soon."

"But what if I do? What if I go to my seat and start working this very minute? Then, can I have him back?"

"Yes, Lester. Yes. Just go sit down."

I grab the packet, run to my desk, and start working right away.

The pretest isn't hard. There are only a few problems on the whole test that I'm not sure of, and even though I started after everyone else, I'm one of the first ones to finish.

After turning in my test, I watch the red second hand make circles around the clock. Not one of my school research books said anything about waiting, but they should have. It seems like that's all we do here.

Once everyone else is finally done, Mrs. Raines says we can talk quietly. I run up to her desk to get Superman, but she tells me I can't have him until after the afternoon announcements.

"Man, that was brutal," the kid across the aisle says to me when I sit down.

His name is Michael, but that's not what we're supposed to call him. Since there are two kids named Michael, Mrs. Raines says we have to call him Michael Z. She says it will keep us from getting them confused with each other. But how could anyone ever get them confused? Michael Z is really short, has dark brown skin, and sits way over here on this side of the room next to me. Michael H is tall, has pinkish skin, and sits way over on the other side of the room behind Ricky.

"Hello?" Michael Z waves his hand in front of his face.

It just feels so strange calling him that, even in my head.

"Lester!"

"What?"

"Stop staring. It's creeping me out."

"I was just thinking how weird it is that we have to call you Michael Z when it's not your name."

"It's kind of my name. You know, Michael Zoss. Michael Z." He shrugs. "As long as no one calls me Mike, it's all good."

The kid on the other side of Michael Z taps him on the shoulder. "You coming to soccer tonight?"

"Oh yeah." Michael Z turns toward him. "We gotta get ready for Ricky's team this weekend. This kid on my bus played his team last week, and they totally got crushed."

I stare at the clock again and wait for the announcements to start. In three minutes, the day will be over, and I can get Superman back. Then I'll go home, and everything will be better.

For now.

But what about tomorrow? I asked Mr. Marmel if I could eat in his office every day, but he said no. He said that I'd get used to the noise. But you can't get used to something that makes your head feel like it's going to explode.

I just can't eat in there. I'll have to go all the way from breakfast to dinner without eating. But I can't do that.

And Mom would never make me! She knows how hungry I get.

Mr. Marmel's voice booms over the speaker. As soon as he's done with the announcements, I zoom up to Mrs. Raines's desk to get Superman.

"I'm not going to see him out during the school day again, right, Lester?"

"Don't worry. You won't see him again."

She hands him to me.

You won't see *me* again either, not after I tell Mom about the cafeteria. I run back to the coat closet and grab my backpack off the hook.

"Looks like baby got his toy back," Ricky says from behind me. Then he grabs Superman and throws him on the ground. "Oops. I dropped him."

"At least it wasn't spaghetti," Connor says, and they both laugh.

I reach down to grab Superman off the ground, but before I do, Ricky steps on him.

Superman! I take him back to my desk.

"Is he okay?" Abby asks.

His arms and legs move. His body twists. His head turns. His cape is still glued on at the top.

"He's fine," I tell Abby.

I stuff Superman deep down in my pocket where he'll be safe. I'm never letting him get close to Ricky ever again.

The bell rings and everyone lines up.

None of it matters now. Once I tell Mom that I can't eat

at school, I'll never have to see any of these people ever again.

In the hallway, our class splits in two. The bus riders go right and the car riders go left.

"Bye, Lester," Abby says, and waves as she turns toward the buses.

I turn in the opposite direction and follow the rest of the car riders to the front of the school. When I get outside, Mom's car is first in line. A teacher yells at me to stop running, but I'll never see her again either.

"How was your first day?" Mom asks as soon as I open the door. "Mine was great!"

"I can't eat here."

"What?"

The car behind us honks.

"Buckle up so we can go home."

"I can't eat here, Mom, and fifth graders don't get snack, which means if I come back tomorrow I'll be too hungry."

"What are you talking about?"

"You know what it's like when I'm really hungry?"

"Yes."

"Well, that's what it was like, Mom. I waited so long for lunch. Then I waited longer because there was only one lady serving food. Then I waited even longer because the cafeteria was so loud I had to put my fingers in my ears and my tray dropped and I didn't get to eat until I was in the principal's office and the front desk lady—"

The car behind us honks again.

Mom grabs my seatbelt and clicks it closed around me. We pull out of the car rider line and into a parking spot.

"You were in the principal's office, Lester?"

"Yes, and it was quiet enough for me to eat in there, but he said I had to eat in the cafeteria from now on."

She reaches over and tucks the hair behind my ear like she used to when I was little. "Do you remember when we moved here? Remember how much you hated it at first? It was so different from our house in Florida. But then you found things you liked about Indiana. Like snow. And your big room with your desk and bookcases. And how dark the sky gets here at night."

"These are not things I can learn to like, Mom."

"School is just different, and it's going to take a little while to adjust." She takes my hand. "Didn't anything good happen today?"

I think for a minute. "This girl named Abby said she liked my name."

"Maybe you two will end up being friends."

"No, we won't because I can't eat lunch there, remember? And if I can't eat at school, I can't go to school."

"I knew you had trouble with thunder and fireworks, but who would have thought a school cafeteria would be so loud?" She leans her head back against the seat. "What if I could make it quieter in there, Lester?"

"You can't, Mom. The cafeteria lady said it's always that loud. And besides, I had to wait so long to get food that my stomach felt like it was eating itself."

"But if I could fix those things, then everything would be fine. Right?"

She doesn't wait for me to answer. She just turns on the car and drives us straight to the store. We get a lunchbox so I won't have to wait in the long lunch line, eggs and bacon so I can have more protein for breakfast and won't get so hungry, and earplugs that I can wear in the cafeteria so my head doesn't feel like it's going to explode.

Mom thinks it's all going to help. She tells me I'm going to be fine.

Again.

But when I'm at school, I'm the opposite of fine. And there's nothing Mom can buy at the store to change that.

School. Again.

MOM PULLS UP TO THE CURB IN FRONT OF SCHOOL. "DO YOU have your lunchbox?"

"Yes."

"And your earplugs?"

I check the outside pocket of my lunchbox. All three pairs are there. My regular pair. My backup pair. And my backup-backup pair.

"See? You're all ready." Mom pats my leg. "If you want, I can park and come in with you."

She came in with me yesterday, and that didn't help. "Mom, I think I'm sick."

"Lester, you're not sick."

"I might be." I take her hand and put it against my forehead.

"Nope."

"Sometimes you can be sick without a fever."

"It's going to be better today." Mom squeezes my hand. "I know it is."

When I get to my classroom, Ricky and Connor aren't there yet, so I hang up my backpack as fast as I can and sit down.

I put my lunchbox under my desk like Abby did yesterday and check the little pocket on the outside to make sure my earplugs are still there.

Then I check the schedule. Mrs. Raines told us that she'd write a schedule on the board so we know exactly what we'll be doing every day. I read down through the list of classes. It's mostly the same as yesterday with spelling, reading, and writing in the morning, but the afternoon is different. Math is shorter today, and after math is SCIENCE!

We're doing science today! And Mrs. Raines is my teacher now, not Mom, and if she likes studying outer space, well, that could change everything—in the best way possible. Mom and I never study space together because it makes her think of Dad. She lets me check out books about space, but we never talk about them or do any space things except once a year when we watch the meteor shower.

I run up to Mrs. Raines's desk. "How do you feel about space?"

"Good morning, Lester."

"How do you feel about space?" I ask again.

"I'm pretty sure I'm pro space. Because, let's face it, if space didn't exist then neither would we."

"No, I mean *studying* space. You know, like the planets and the moon and stars? Are we going to study space this year?"

"The fifth grade does a huge space unit every spring, and actually, it's my second-favorite unit of the year."

"What's your first-favorite?" Please don't say plants. Please don't say plants.

She puts her hand on her chest. "Simple machines hold a very special place in my heart."

"Do plants hold a special place in your heart too?" Mom loves plants, which means we studied them. Every. Single. Year.

"I like plants in salads, Lester, but not so much in my curriculum."

"What's curriculum?"

"Just a fancy word for the things we study in school. See Lester, the younger kids study plants. A lot. So we get to focus on the fun stuff. Simple machines. Properties of matter. Reactions."

"And space?"

"Yup. There's a whole chapter in your science book about it."

I had a book in my desk all day yesterday with the chapter about space in it, and I didn't know it?

"Hi, Lester," Abby says when I get back to my desk.

I open my book to the table of contents and run my finger down the page. Chapter nine: Stars and Planets.

"Did you know we get to study space this year, Abby?"

"Yeah," Abby says. "In the spring, the fifth graders always have a space fair for the rest of the school. Last year there were giant models of the planets. The year before that, I think they did a play about the constellations or something."

"Remember when they brought this blow-up dome thing into the gym, and we got to go inside and look at the stars?" Michael Z asks.

"You had a planetarium *here*? In the actual school?"

"Yeah, I remember the planetarium!" Abby says. "How old were we?"

"First grade, I think," Michael Z says.

I turn to chapter nine and there it is.

A whole chapter about space in my science book? A space fair in the spring? And a whole year without doing one plant experiment? This might just turn out to be the best year ever.

Right then, Ricky, Connor, and a bunch of other kids walk into the room. It sounds like someone multiplied the noise in here by eight.

"Boys!" Mrs. Raines says from her desk. "Lower your voices. You are in a classroom now."

The room gets quieter right away.

Mrs. Raines should be in the cafeteria telling the kids in there to be quiet too. But she's not—which means the earplugs are my only hope. If they don't work, I'll never make it to science.

Earplugs

WHEN MRS. RAINES TELLS US TO LINE UP FOR LUNCH, I ROLL MY earplugs between my fingers and stick them in my ears. In a few seconds, they puff up and everything gets quieter, just like it did when I practiced using them last night.

They seem to be working so far, but I'm not in the cafeteria yet. I'm still in my classroom, and it's already quiet in here.

The class walks in a single-file line to the cafeteria, just like we did yesterday, but we seem to get there so much faster today.

Abby opens the door. "Since you brought your lunch, you can come in here with me today."

The noise coming from inside the cafeteria sounds like a low faraway buzz. But maybe that's because I'm in the hallway. It could still get louder inside.

"Come on," Abby says, and walks through the door.

I follow her in and . . . nothing changes. "Abby! They work!"

"What works?"

"Quick, Abby! Say something else."

"What?"

"I can even hear you talk with them in!"

"With what in, Lester?"

"My earplugs." I take one out to show her, but as soon as I do, the swirling noise fills my head. I shove it right back into my ear. "I have to keep them in or else my head feels like it's going to explode from all the noise."

"Really?" Abby pokes at one of them but doesn't pull it out.

"Yeah. How can you stand it in here?"

Abby shrugs. "It's loud, but it doesn't really bother me."

We sit down across from each other at the end of one of the tables and unpack our lunches. I eat my cookie first since Mom's not here to make me save it for the end.

"So, what's your style, Lester?" Abby asks me.

"What's style?" I ask.

"You know, fashion—what kinds of clothes you wear, what trends you like. Like how last year everyone wore sweats so sweats were the trend."

"I like sweats."

"Well, you can't wear them this year. Sweats were so fourth grade." Abby takes a bite of her sandwich. "If you could wear anything, what would it be?"

"My Superman suit," I tell her before I even have a chance to think about it. "But it doesn't fit anymore. I used to wear it when I was little."

Abby stares real hard at me like she's trying to look straight into my brain.

"Yes. Yes. I'm seeing it now."

"Seeing what?"

She pulls a shiny pink notebook and pencil from her back pocket and starts drawing. "Skinny jeans. Vintage T-shirt. Maybe a little cape?" She draws some more. "Add the perfect shoes, and there you have it."

"What do I have?"

She holds up the notebook so I can see her drawing. "Superhero chic!"

"Superhero chic?" The word *chic* makes me feel like I'm talking in a different language.

"What'd you say, Mouse Boy?" Ricky says from down the table. "I can't hear you."

Ricky and Connor are holding carrots up to their ears.

"Why do you have carrots in your ears?" I ask.

"Um . . . ," Ricky says really slowly. "Why do you?"

The earplugs. They're orange! I pull one out to show Ricky that it's not a carrot at all, but the noise comes swirling in again. I can't take the earplugs out in here. Ever.

Abby turns toward them. "Leave him alone, Ricky."

"Why don't you come and make me, Abby *Double*-Chin?"

All the kids at the table stare at Abby. Her face turns the same color as her notebook.

Just then, a bell rings.

Abby shoves everything into her lunchbox and runs across the room to a door with a red *Exit* sign above it. So do Ricky and Connor and the rest of the kids at the table. That must be how you get to the playground.

I finish my sandwich in two bites and follow them. It's my first recess ever, and I know exactly what I want to do.

As soon as I step outside, I take out one earplug, then the other. Even though kids are screaming and yelling all around me, it's so big and open out here that the noise doesn't bother me at all.

When I get to the swings, all of them are taken. Five by kids who are actually swinging, and one by Abby. She's just sitting on it.

"Are you going to swing?" I ask her.

"What does it look like?"

"It looks like you're sitting there and not swinging."

"That's right."

I grab onto the chain. "Can I use it, then? You could sit and not swing anywhere but I can only swing right here."

"Why are you being so mean to me when I just stood up for you?"

When did she stand up for me? "You mean when Ricky

66

called you Abby Double-Chin and you *stood up* and ran out the doors?"

"Lester!" Abby says.

"What?"

Tori, the girl on the swings next to Abby, stops swinging and stares at us.

"What are you looking at?" Abby says to Tori.

Tori gets up and runs away.

A free swing! I sit down and pump my legs. Back and forth. Higher and higher. Just like I'm flying.

"Brooke always knew exactly what to say whenever someone was mean to us."

"Who's Brooke?" I ask.

"My best friend." Abby leans her head against the chain. "She moved away last summer."

"I've never had a best friend," I tell Abby.

Abby watches me swing by a few more times, then she starts swinging too. When she gets high enough, her long black hair flies straight out behind her.

"I wish my hair was like yours."

"What are you talking about, Lester?"

"When you swing, it flies out behind you like a cape. It's like you get to wear a cape all the time."

Abby swings even higher.

I pump to keep up.

SCIENCE!!!!!!

SCIENCE WAS SUPPOSED TO START FIVE MINUTES AGO. THAT'S what the schedule said. But the kids who go to the other fifth grade teacher's room for math aren't back and the kids who came to our classroom haven't left yet. It's like no one even cares about science!

I raise my hand again. "Mrs. Raines, it's 2:20."

"All right. If you're in Mrs. Turner's class, you can head back now. And don't forget your homework is due tomorrow before the morning bell."

The kids from Mrs. Turner's class leave, and some of the kids from our room come back. But not all of them. There are still five empty desks.

That's it. I'm starting without them. I grab my science book out of my desk and open to the space chapter.

When Mrs. Raines finally walks up to the front of the room, we've already missed ten minutes of my first science class of the year. "That transition was slower than molasses," she says. "We're going to have to speed it up or we'll never get to history."

"You mean science," I tell her.

"That's right. Our last class of the day will be either history or science. Now, raise your hand if you know what a timeline is."

Most of the kids raise their hands. I raise mine, too, because Mom and I used to do them all the time. But that was always in history. We've never used one in science before.

Mrs. Raines draws a long line across the whiteboard. "Since we're focusing on the United States this year, we're going to start by recording all the historical events we already know."

Historical events?

Mrs. Raines writes three dates on the timeline. "Who can tell me what happened in 1776?"

A bunch of kids raise their hands.

"That sounds like history."

"That's because it is," Mrs. Raines says to me.

"But we're supposed to be having science right now. It says so on the schedule."

Mrs. Raines walks over to the schedule board, erases *Science*, and writes *History*.

"You can't change it!"

"It's not really a change, Lester. I just wrote the wrong subject this morning."

"But I've been waiting all day."

Some kids laugh, but I don't care, not even a little bit. The schedule said we were having science so that's what I'm going to do. I grab my book and stand up.

"Lester, sit down."

"Are we having science?"

"No. I told you—"

I run out of the room and down the hall.

Mrs. Raines yells for me to come back.

But I'm not going to make some stupid history timeline when I'm supposed to be having my first science class of the year.

When I get to the library, I squeeze into the little nook between the two bookshelves in the nonfiction section and open my book to the space chapter.

"This is the second time you've run away from your classroom, Lester," Mr. Marmel says. He's standing in front of me with his arms crossed.

"Last time I ran away from the cafeteria, not my class."

Mr. Marmel shakes his head. "You're not allowed to leave your classroom without permission."

"The whole day the schedule said we were going to do science, but Mrs. Raines changed it to history at the very last minute. I'm just going to have science down here and go back when I'm done."

"You can't do that."

"Why not?"

"Lester, stand up."

"No." My voice bounces off the library walls and back into my ears. I didn't mean for it to be that loud.

Mr. Marmel grabs the book off the floor in front of me. "If you don't stand up and come with me right now, you will never have another science class again."

I squeeze out from between the bookshelves and stand up as fast as I can.

"Now, march yourself straight to my office."

"You want me to *march*?"

"Yes."

"Why?"

"Don't make this worse than it already is, Lester. March. Now." He points toward the library doors.

Even though it doesn't make any sense at all, I have to do what he says or I'll never have science again. So, I swing my arms and lift my knees and act like I'm leading a parade straight out the library doors and into the hallway.

"What in the world are you doing?" He steps in front of me.

"Marching."

He's breathing so hard I can actually see his shoulders

moving up and down. "You think this is all some big joke, don't you?"

It doesn't feel like a joke. It feels like the opposite of a joke.

"Look at me when I'm talking to you!" His voice screams into my ears.

I stare down at the specks of blue in the gray carpet.

"Lester."

Blue specks. And white specks. And green specks.

"Look at me, Lester!" he yells.

So, I do it. I look him right in the eye and he looks right back at me and my brain starts jumping around just like I knew it would . . . to the library . . . to him yelling . . . to me marching . . . to him telling me to look him in the eye . . . then back to the library again . . . then more yelling . . . I just . . . I can't do this anymore . . . if I don't look away soon, my brain is going to burst into a million pieces.

I reach out for the wall behind me and slide down until I'm on the floor. I pull my knees into my chest, bury my face between them, and rock.

Back and forth.

Back and forth.

Back and forth.

Finally, my brain gets quiet and everything feels far away.

"I have to do the afternoon announcements in a few minutes," Mr. Marmel says. His voice is quieter. "Why don't you come wait in my office, and we can talk after that."

I don't move. Mr. Marmel's office is the last place I want to be.

"Here." He holds my science book out to me. "You can read this while you're waiting."

Waiting

THE OFFICE DOOR SWINGS OPEN. MR. MARMEL WALKS AROUND his desk and sits down. A second later, Mom walks through the door.

"What are you doing here?" I ask.

She sits down on one of the wooden chairs in front of Mr. Marmel's desk. "Come over here and tell me what happened, Lester."

I pull a chair from the table over to where Mom is sitting. "We were supposed to be having science. I waited the whole day for it. But Mrs. Raines changed the schedule right at the last minute, so I went to the library to have my own science."

"Was your teacher with you?"

I know the real answer isn't the one Mom wants to hear.

"Lester . . ."

"No."

"You always have to stay with your teacher. That's how you stay safe."

"But I just went to the library, Mom!"

Mr. Marmel leans across the desk. "Are you telling me you really didn't know you weren't allowed to go to the library, alone, in the middle of history class?"

"I spend time by myself in the library where Mom works. And at home if I want to do a different subject, we just do."

He writes something down. "What about when I told you to march and you acted like you were in a parade?"

"I was just doing what you told me to do!"

"Lester," Mom says, "marching can mean just going some-where quickly. It doesn't always mean the parade kind of marching."

She looks at Mr. Marmel. "He's always been kind of literal."

Mr. Marmel writes something else on his notepad. "Since you seem to be having trouble with the rules—"

"What rules?" I wipe the tears out of my eyes. "I don't even know what the rules are here!"

Mom scoots her chair closer to mine and rubs circles on my back.

"I know," Mr. Marmel says. "That's why we're going to write them out for you, Lester. When you leave tonight, you'll have a list of rules that you need to follow while you're at school. Does that sound like something you can do?"

"Yes. I'm really good at following rules when I know what they are."

Mr. Marmel opens the lid of his laptop. "Rule 1: Stay with your teacher at all times. That seems to be our biggest issue at the moment."

I raise my hand. "What about when I have to go to the bathroom? How can I stay with my teacher then?"

Mr. Marmel looks up at the ceiling and takes a breath before looking back down at his computer.

"I know! We could make the rule: Stay with your teacher at all times, except when you're going to the bathroom."

"Would that be easier for you to follow?" he asks.

"Well, yeah, because I can't follow the other one at all."

He types some more. "Next we need a rule about following directions. Let's say: Do what my teacher says, when she says to do it." He keeps making up more and more rules. About not arguing and not speaking unless I raise my hand and my teacher calls on me. And then there's an important one about never ever running away even if I'm really upset.

When he finishes, there are ten rules in all. He clicks a button and a piece of paper comes out of the printer behind him. "Now that you know the rules, I expect you to follow them."

"I will," I tell him. And I really mean it. Science is all about following rules and I'm really good at science, which means I'll be good at following these rules, too.

The Rules

AFTER MOM FINISHES CLEARING THE DINNER DISHES OFF THE
table, she sits down with the list of rules. Again.

"Mom! We've studied them every night for a whole week."

"Let's just go through them one more time."

"But I already know them all. Rule 1: Stay with a teacher at
all times, except when going to the bathroom. Rule 2: Do what
my teacher says to do when she says to do it. Rule 3:—"

Mom puts the paper back on the refrigerator with a mag-
net. "You're following them at school, right?"

"Yes."

She shakes her head.

"I am!"

"I know you are. I'm just not there to see it. Sometimes I

feel like I'm missing everything in your life now."

"That's because you got a job and made me go to school."

"Yeah," Mom says, and stares off into the living room. Then she gets this really big smile on her face. "I didn't even tell you what happened yet. You know how I've been working at the circulation desk, checking books in and out, reshelving materials, and that kind of thing? Well, the adult services librarian—"

"Miss Karen?"

"Right. I forgot you knew her name. Anyway, Karen was out sick today and they asked me to fill in for her. Me, Lester."

"You got to be like Miss Jamie, but for the adults."

"And that's not even the best part. Garret, who works in receiving, told me that Karen wasn't actually sick today. He said she was interviewing for a job at a college in Indianapolis. Do you know what that means?"

"No."

"It means that if she leaves, I could maybe get her position. Imagine that, Lester. *Lucy Musselbaum, Adult Services. What can I help you with today?*" Mom looks up over my head like she's actually talking to someone at the library. "I know that a lot of people have been working there longer than me, but I think I'm the most qualified."

"What about me?"

"Since you're ten and you didn't go to school to be a librarian, I don't think I have to worry about you stealing the job away from me," Mom says, and laughs.

But that's not what I was talking about. Mom's just . . . she's acting so weird. The last time she talked this much about something, it was the rules. Or going to school. Or something else to do with me.

I grab my backpack off the hook by the door. "Mom, I have homework. And we need to do it now."

"I'm getting my hopes up too high, aren't I? We don't even know if she's leaving yet." Mom moves across the table so she's sitting beside me. "What do we have tonight?"

"A reading worksheet." I pull the paper out of my backpack.

Mom looks at it. "We better read the story before we try to answer these questions."

"We read it in class today."

She hands the paper back to me. "Then go ahead."

I read question one, but I can't remember the answer. I can't remember the answers for questions two or three either. Or four. Or five.

"I need my book, Mom."

"Where is it?"

"At school. We have to go get it."

"It's after seven, Lester. The school won't be open now."

"But doing my homework is a rule." I grab the paper off the fridge and point to *Rule 5: Complete all work and turn it in on time.* "It has to be turned in tomorrow morning before the bell!"

Think brain, think. I sit back down and stare at the questions. But the harder I think, the less I can remember the story.

"Can we go to the library?" I ask Mom.

"We could, but I know we don't have your reading book there. It's a special kind of book they only have at schools."

Tomorrow morning when I walk into my classroom, Mrs. Raines will remind us to turn in our homework like she always does. And everyone else will walk up to her desk and drop their paper in the tray, everyone except me. Then Mrs. Raines will go through the papers and ask me where my homework is and why I don't have it done and—

"Lester, settle down. I just thought of something. Well, half of something."

"What?"

"You might be able to borrow a book from someone in your class."

"Is that allowed?"

"Yeah, but the problem is, we don't have a school directory so I don't have anyone's phone number."

Mom may not have anyone's number, but I do. I reach in my pocket and pull out Abby's sparkly pink card. "I have Abby's number right here."

Abby's House

THE HOUSES ON ABBY'S STREET ARE ALL BIG AND MADE OF GRAY stone. At the end of the street, on a big paved circle area, we finally find the house number Abby's mom told us. A window on the second floor is glowing pink. I'm pretty sure I know which room is Abby's.

Mom rings the doorbell.

A few seconds later a woman answers the door. "Come in, come in!"

She looks a lot like Abby except that her stomach is really big and round. We follow her inside to a square room where the ceiling is as tall as the whole house. There are plastic blocks and colored rings and stuffed animals all over the floor. She kicks the toys out of the way as we walk through.

"Sorry about the mess. My husband's away on business right now and I'm in no state to be cleaning." The little kid crawling across the floor stops when he gets to her feet. "Isn't that right, Bo?" She leans over, holding her stomach with her right hand, and grabs the little kid.

"Abby, your friend's here," she yells up the stairs.

Abby's face pops over the edge of the banister. "Hey, Lester! Come up and see my room."

"Can I?" I ask Mom. I've never been in someone else's room before.

"Go ahead."

"I need to sit down," Abby's mom says. She walks into the next room and plops down on the couch. "Care to join me?" she asks Mom.

Mom walks over to the couch, and I walk up the stairs. We used to have stairs at our house in Florida, but not as many as there are here.

As soon as I get upstairs, I can tell I was right about which room was Abby's. The walls are striped with two pinks; one is the color of bubble gum, and the other is darker reddish pink like the peonies in our yard.

"I couldn't figure out which color I liked better so we had the painters do both."

There's a giant bulletin board on the wall with drawings and magazine cut-outs and pieces of cloth. Her desk is covered with piles of magazines and papers and colored pencils. It's not neat and organized like her desk is at school.

Just then, a girl who looks like Abby but shorter runs into the room, grabs something off Abby's desk, and runs back out.

"Caroline!" Abby yells.

A door slams down the hallway.

"Mom! Caroline's taking my stuff again!"

She turns back to me. "I hope the next one's a boy."

"What next one?"

"My mom's pregnant, Lester. Couldn't you tell? She's giant."

I noticed her stomach was big. I didn't know that meant there was a baby in it.

"My reading book's on my dresser," Abby says, and points across her room. "I'm going to get my colored pencil back."

If Abby isn't in here, then I don't need to be in here either, which is good because all the pink is starting to hurt my eyes. I grab the reading book off her dresser, but stop when I notice what's next to it—a golden statue of a kid holding a telescope and looking up to the sky. It looks like something that should be in my room, not Abby's. The statue is standing up on a little piece of wood, and on the front of the wood, there's a gold plate that says: *Quarry Elementary Junior Scientist. Abby Chin.*

I grab the statue off her dresser and run out into the hallway. "Abby!"

She walks out of the room at the end of the hall holding a colored pencil.

"What is this, Abby?"

"Oh. That's just my science fair trophy."

"What's a science fair?"

"Just this thing we do at school where we create science projects. Then judges come in and pick the best one."

"How did you get this trophy?"

"I won last year."

"I didn't know you could win science!" I rub my finger over Abby's name. "Does our school have a science fair every year?"

"Yup."

"Does everyone get to do it?"

"Just the fourth and fifth graders."

"I'm a fifth grader!"

Abby laughs. "I know that, Lester."

What Abby doesn't know is that I already have the perfect idea for a project. I found it on the computer over a year ago, and now it's in my secret ideas folder in my bottom dresser drawer under my snow pants where Mom never looks.

But I don't have to hide it because Mom's not my teacher anymore. Mrs. Raines is, and I bet she's going to love it.

A Question

I WALK AS FAST AS I CAN WITHOUT BREAKING *RULE 8: NO running in the school building.* When I get to the classroom, Mrs. Raines is sitting at her desk stapling green papers together.

"I have an idea for my project," I tell Mrs. Raines.

"You mean the partner poems we started yesterday?"

"No, my science fair project."

"But I didn't tell you about the science fair yet. Wait. Did I?" She flips through a notebook.

"No. I was at Abby's house last night and saw her trophy." I pull my secret folder out of my bag. "This experiment is—"

"Oh good. For a second, I thought I was losing it." Mrs. Raines leans back in her chair and looks at me. "You have really good timing, you know."

"No. I don't know that. Why do I have good timing?"

"I'm stapling the science fair packets together right now. And we're going to talk about it this afternoon in science." She points to the board. For the first time since Mrs. Raines wrote it by mistake, it says *science* on the schedule.

When math is finally over, I walk up to Mrs. Raines's desk. "Are we—"

"For the hundredth time, Lester, yes, we are having science today, and yes, we are talking about the science fair."

"You're sure?"

"Lester!"

"I'm just afraid you might change your mind and tell us we're doing a history fair instead."

She picks up the large stack of green papers from the corner of her desk. "Now that you mention it, a history fair does sound like a great idea. Think of all the historical things you'd learn."

"No! You can't change it!"

"Lester."

Even though I just found out about it yesterday, I feel like I've been waiting for the science fair my whole life.

"Lester, I'm joking." She shows me the top of the stack of papers. It says: *Quarry Elementary Science Fair Informational Packet.*

That wasn't a very funny joke. I cross my arms and try to

be mad at her, but I can't because any second she's going to walk up to the front of the room and start telling us about the science fair and—

It's starting. Science is starting!

"As you know, we've been focusing on history for the first week and a half of school," Mrs. Raines says. "But I think it's about time we switched things up."

"Yeah!" I yell.

"And today marks our grand departure into science fair projects."

Some of the kids slouch down in their chairs and make noises like they have stomachaches. But not me. I sit up as straight as I can and keep myself completely quiet so I can focus on every single word she's saying.

"As most of you know, a science fair project is basically just a science experiment that you do on your own. You will choose a topic that interests you, design your own experiment, and test a hypothesis using the scientific method."

"Can we really choose any topic?" I ask.

"Lester, you need to raise your hand."

I know. I know. Rule 4. I put my hand in the air.

"Yes, Lester."

"Can we really choose any topic?"

"Yes, as long as it's testable."

"What about flying? Can I do an experiment about that?"

She scrunches up her face. "Possibly. But you would

probably need to do some research first."

"It's all right here." I grab the papers out of the folder and run up to Mrs. Raines to show her. "See? Flying and aerodynamics and types of paper airplanes. I'm going to test different wing shapes and see which shape helps the airplanes go the farthest."

She takes the papers from me and looks through them. The room is quiet. Everyone's looking at me, but this time, I don't care. If I get to do this project, I'm going to have to get used to people looking at me. When you win something this important, you get sort of famous and everyone wants to talk to you.

"Well, you've certainly done your research, Lester. And actually, I think your experiment sounds great." She hands my papers back to me. "It's testable. It's scientific. You really seem to care about it." She looks out at the class. "That is the most important part."

The experiment has been sitting there in my secret folder for over a year. I knew Mom wouldn't let me do it. She says no every time I want to do a project about space or flying or anything that makes her think of Dad. But now I get to, and it's all because of Mrs. Raines.

I reach out and give her a big hug.

"I guess we know who'll win the prize for most enthusiastic," Mrs. Raines says, and pats my back.

I let go of her. "There's a prize for winning AND a prize

for most enthusiastic?" I'm not just going to win one prize, I'm going to win two!

"Actually, no, Lester. I . . . wait a second." She reaches inside her tall angled desk, which I learned last week is called a podium, and opens a little plastic envelope with sheets of gold stars in it. She peels one off and sticks it to my shirt.

"This is for being so enthusiastic, Lester. But now you need to go sit down because I need to explain everything else."

I run back to my desk and listen to every word she says. After explaining how we choose a topic and design the experiment and draw a conclusion and make the board, Mrs. Raines hands out a packet with all the information on it. On the very back page is a place for us to write down our research question. Mrs. Raines says we have to turn them in by the end of next week. But I don't need to wait until then. I already know exactly what my experiment is, and Mrs. Raines already said I could do it.

I write *What shape of wing helps paper airplanes fly the farthest?* on my form, tear the page off the back of my packet, and bring it up to Mrs. Raines.

She looks at it for a second. "This looks great," she says. But then she holds it out to me like she's trying to give it back.

"Should I put it in the tray?"

"Not yet." She points to something at the bottom of the page that says *parent signature*. "Your mom needs to sign it first."

"I can't ask my mom. She'll say no!"

"Then you'll need to think of another experiment."

No. No, no, no. I feel the tears in the corners of my eyes.

"Lester, I'm sorry—"

"But she's not my teacher anymore. You are. And you already said I could do it."

"Parents have to approve all science fair projects, Lester. That's a rule."

"You mean if my mom doesn't sign the paper I don't have to do it?" Ricky asks from across the room.

Connor and some of the other kids laugh.

Mrs. Raines crosses her arms. "Sure, Ricky and all of you others who think that idea is so funny. Just be sure to mention to your parents that this project is worth fifty percent of your grade, and if you don't do it, you'll fail science this quarter."

They all stop laughing.

Mrs. Raines hands the paper back to me. "These projects have to be done outside of school, so they have to be something your parents are willing to help you with. That's why we need the signature."

Mom'll say no. I know she will. And then I'll end up having to do another experiment about dumb old plants.

When I get back to my desk, Michael Z is talking to Sydney, the girl who sits in front of him, about magnets. He'll probably write down his experiment, hand the paper to his mom, and she'll sign it without asking any questions.

I kick my desk leg, and it hits the back of Abby's chair.

She turns around. "Can you stop?"

I kick it again.

"Lester!"

She doesn't understand. She already has a trophy.

Mrs. Raines dismisses us to get our things ready to go home. Abby stands up and scoots her chair under her desk so it's really far away from me.

Ricky stops next to my desk. "Nice star, Mouse Boy."

Mom said he just calls me that to make me upset. Well, he can try all he wants, but there's no way I could be more upset than I am right now.

Connor walks up behind him. "Aww, wook, Connow," Ricky says, and leans his face down, right next to my ear. "Wittle baby is mad."

"Maybe hugging Mrs. Waines again would hewp," Connor says.

"Ricky. Connor." Mrs. Raines stands up. "That's a warning."

I bury my head on my desk. All I want is to do my science experiment—to fold paper airplanes with different wing shapes and throw them and measure distances and come up with a conclusion about what I discover. That's all.

"You didn't ask her yet," Abby says.

"What?" I say into my desk.

"You didn't ask your mom yet. Maybe she'll let you do it."

Abby doesn't know my mom like I do. If she did, she'd know what I know.

There's no way Mom will ever say yes.

Permission

I'VE BEEN TRYING TO THINK OF THE RIGHT WORDS FOR ALMOST a week, the ones that will make Mom let me do my airplane experiment. But there are no right words. It's just like I told Abby. Mom will never say yes.

I stare up at my ceiling and fly Superman around in circles.

Mom knocks on my door frame. "Since you're already in bed, I think I'll go finish my book in my bedroom. Let me know when you're ready to be tucked in."

The paper is due in thirteen hours. This is my last chance.

"Mom, wait. Can you go sit on the couch for a minute?"

"Why?"

"I need to talk to you."

"Is something wrong?"

"No." Not yet. Not until I ask her.

"Are you sure? You've got Superman out."

"Just go in the living room. I'll be there in a second."

She turns around and walks out.

I grab the paper and follow her. When I get out there, I sit down on the couch and put the paper upside down on my lap.

Okay.

I'm going to do it now.

I'm going to ask her.

"Lester?"

"What?"

"Are you sure there's nothing wr—"

"You're not my teacher anymore."

"Did something happen at school today?"

I stare down at the green paper. "Since you're not my teacher, that means you're not supposed to tell me what I can and can't do science experiments about."

"When did I tell you that you couldn't do a science experiment about something?"

"You didn't. But I know you will. I didn't even want to tell you about it, but Mrs. Raines said you have to sign the paper with my research question on it or I can't do the project."

"Is this the paper?"

I nod.

She takes the paper off my lap and looks at it. It feels like it takes her an hour to read that one little line.

"You want to do an experiment about flying?"

"Yes."

"Why?"

"Because I love flying."

"Is this because of Superman?"

"No."

"Is this because of your dad?"

"I don't know."

She hands the paper back to me. "Anything but flying."

"What about space, then?"

"Lester . . ."

"But space and flying are what I love the most. They're what I want to learn about and read about, and most of all, they're what I want to do experiments about."

She tries to get down low so she can look me in the eyes, but I keep my eyes fixed on the carpet.

"I don't understand why you have to be interested in such dangerous things, Lester."

"My experiment isn't dangerous. I'm just going to be throwing some paper airplanes and measuring how far they go. I'm not actually going to be flying."

"But this is where it starts. Don't you see? First, you'll do this experiment for the science fair. Then you'll learn more about it in middle school next year, and in high school, and then you'll want to take an aerospace engineering class in college." She leans over on her knees. "Just like your dad."

"Aerospace engineering. That's a class about space *and* flying, right?"

"Yes, but that's not—"

"Did Dad do experiments in the class? Like how I do experiments?"

"Lester!"

"*You're* the one who started talking about him."

"Because I was trying to explain to you why this experiment is a bad idea. Do you know what he said to me, Lester?"

How would I know what Dad said when she never tells me anything about him? We never talk about Dad.

"'It's just a class, Lucy, I'm not actually going into space.'" That's what he *said*. She looks right into my eyes. "But do you know what he did?"

I do know. I know exactly what he did. And I know what happened. I also know how sad Mom gets about it. But this time I'm not going to try to make her feel better because no matter how hard I try the sadness just keeps coming back over and over and over again, and this time, it's going to ruin my project.

"What about me, Mom? What about what I want to do? I'm not doing another dumb experiment about plants." I run into my room and I slam my door. Hard. And punch the pillow on my bed.

I knew she'd be like this.

Punch.

I knew she wouldn't let me do it.

Punch.

She never lets me do anything I want to do.

Punch.

Punch.

Punch.

Promise

"LESTER?" MOM'S HAND IS ON MY SHOULDER.

My room is dark except for my bedside lamp.

She sits down on the edge of my bed, holding the green paper and a pen. "This is just a science experiment, right?"

I sit up and face her. "Right."

"You're not going to become an airplane pilot or something?"

"Ten-year-olds can't be pilots, Mom."

"No, I mean in the future. Promise me you will never become an airplane pilot."

"I promise I will never be an airplane pilot."

"Or an astronaut."

"Mom . . ."

"Lester, I'm just trying to keep you safe. As your mom, that's my job. Don't you want to stay safe so you can live a long, happy life?"

"Right now, I just want to do my airplane experiment."

"And you can, if you just promise me that you'll never become an astronaut."

I close my eyes and try to think. Do I even want to be an astronaut? I don't even know what that would be like.

"Lester." She holds the pen up. "Promise me."

"Fine. I promise never to become an astronaut."

She takes the pen and writes her name on the line at the bottom. In ink. Unerasable ink.

"Now get ready for bed. It's already after nine, and you've got school in the morning."

I put on my pajamas, turn off my light, and wait.

At 9:32, when Mom's light finally goes off, I sit down at my desk and open my lab notebook. It's time to plan my experiment.

Planning

AT LUNCH, I SIT DOWN NEXT TO ABBY INSTEAD OF IN MY NOR-mal spot across from her. That way when I show her my lab notebook, we'll both be looking at it right side up.

"I stayed up extra late, but I got my experiment all planned out."

She looks at the pages for a second and then back to her food.

"Don't you want to read it?"

"Lester, I'm eating." She takes a bite of apple.

"Then I'll just explain it to you while you eat. Do you remember my research question from this morning?"

"You mean the one on the paper your mom signed?" Abby says, even though she's chewing and you're not supposed to talk with food in your mouth. "I think everyone in class saw that paper, Lester."

"Then you know I'm going to be testing paper airplane wing shapes. My hypothesis is that planes with the widest wings will go the farthest. Do you want to know how I thought of it?"

"I guess."

"Because of birds, Abby! The birds with the biggest wings always seem to soar the longest, and the birds with the smallest wings don't soar much at all."

"Actually, that does make sense, Lester."

Of course it makes sense. Everything about this experiment makes sense, and it's all right here in my notebook. My research question. My hypothesis. The materials I'm going to need. My procedure. The only thing I don't know yet is where I'm going to launch my planes from.

The lunch lady who pushed me out into the cafeteria the other day stops and wipes something sticky off the table in front of us.

"Is that your lunch?" She points to my lab notebook.

Why would she ask me that? Notebooks are made of paper, not food.

"He was just showing me the plans for his science fair project," Abby says.

The lady crosses her arms. "When that recess bell rings, he has to leave whether he's done eating or not. So I suggest he save the science for science class and eat now. If not, I might just have to take his little notebook."

I close my notebook and set it on the bench between Abby and me. She can't take it. Except for Superman, it's the most important thing in the whole world.

I start eating, and the lunch lady finally walks away.

"What's her problem?" Abby asks.

"The other day she said she hated the noise in here, too. Maybe she needs a pair of earplugs."

"Or a mouth plug," Abby says.

We both laugh.

When Abby and I walk out the recess doors, the wind whips around the side of the building and blows Abby's hair all around in her face. The wind. It's the one thing that could ruin my experiment.

"Have you heard of variables before?" I ask Abby on our way to the swings.

"Of course I have, Lester. I did win the science fair last—"

"Then you know that the variable in my experiment is wing shape. That's the only thing I can change. If I do the experiment on a day with even a little wind—"

"Lester, I was trying to tell you something."

"About my project?"

"No. About *my* project—you know, the project that *won* the science fair last year."

"Okay, Abby. Tell me."

"It was about whether washing clothes in cold water removed stains as well as washing them in warm water."

"You won the science fair with an experiment about laundry? That's not science-y at all."

"It's chemistry, Lester. And it was very scientific."

"How?" I sit down on one of the swings and start swinging.

Abby sits down on the swing next to me and pumps her legs really hard until she's going even higher than me. "I made identical stains on identical shirts. Then, I washed each kind of stain in cold water and hot water. The only variable I changed was the water temperature. How is that any different from your paper airplane experiment?"

"For one thing, it's way easier. You can do laundry anytime, but I can only do my experiment when the conditions are just right. If there's any wind at all, I won't know whether it's the wings or the wind making my planes fly the different distances."

Abby stops pumping and her swing slows down until it stops. "My dad's in China right now."

The other night at Abby's house, I remember her mom saying that her dad was gone, but I didn't know he was all the way in China. That's really far away, and I think the only way people can get to China from Indiana is by taking an airplane.

I stop swinging. "Are you scared his plane is going to crash?"

Abby turns toward me. "Why would you ask me that?"

"Because flying is dangerous."

"No, it's not. He flies there all the time for his job, and it's always fine. Except right now, it's not because he's over there and the baby is coming soon and . . . what if he doesn't get home in time, Lester? My grandma's supposed to be coming soon, but my mom can barely walk anymore and it's just . . ." Abby kicks her foot in the mulch. "When Bo was born, my mom was up and walking around until the day she went to the hospital to have him. But now, she spends most of the time on the couch sleeping."

"I don't know anything about babies."

Abby wipes her hand across her eyes. "Never mind. Let's talk about something else."

"We don't have to. You can keep talking about your mom if you want."

Abby stands up and walks in a circle around her swing. "I know. Let's talk about your experiment. I mean, it's not very science-y, but we can still talk about it, I guess."

I can't believe she's saying that. My airplane experiment is the most science-y experiment there is.

Abby leans over in my face, smiling really big. "I'm joking, you goon. If there's one thing your experiment is, it's science-y. Everything about you is science-y."

I look up at Abby. "That's the nicest thing anyone's ever said to me."

She laughs. "So, what's the next thing you need to figure out?"

"Where I'm going to stand when I launch the planes. It has to be some place high up and it can't have anything in the way like trees or buildings. It has to be safe, too, or Mom won't let me go there."

Abby looks around. A few seconds later, she takes off running.

"Abby!"

She doesn't stop.

When I'm halfway across the playground, I see where she's going. The curly slide.

It's tall. There's nothing else around it. And Mom can't tell me it's too dangerous because kids climb up it every day and no one ever gets hurt. Abby's climbing it right now.

By the time I get to the slide, she's already at the top.

"What do you think?" she yells down to me.

"It's perfect, Abby."

"Come up!"

I've never been over here by the slide before. It seems a lot taller than it did when I was on the swings. I take a step up. Then another step. The wind is blowing so hard, it feels like it's going to blow me right off this ladder.

"Lester, what are you waiting for?"

I climb back down. "The wind is too strong today."

"No, it's not."

But I know it is. I'm just going to have to wait for that perfect windless day. And when it finally comes, I'll climb the curly slide and launch the airplanes, and Mom will measure the distances.

But how will she do that? You can't use a tape measure by yourself. I tried once and the metal tape came back and slapped me in the face. That means I'll have to come down and help her with the measuring.

But that won't work either. Each plane has to be thrown in the exact same way from the *exact* same spot, which means that once I start launching them I can't move. Someone else needs to be on the ground helping Mom with measuring.

Abby disappears over the edge of the platform, and a few seconds later she's sliding down.

"I need your help with my experiment," I tell her when she's on the ground again.

"You want *my* help?"

"You're the only person I know who's good at science."

"So now I'm good at science? I thought my project wasn't science-y enough for you."

"You're good enough to help with the measuring."

Abby shakes her head. "Lester, I don't even know what to say to you sometimes."

"Say you'll help. Please?"

"When would we do it?"

"We have to wait for a completely still day because any wind . . ."

"I know. Any wind would mess up the variables."

"Right."

"Well, it depends on how my mom's doing and if she's had the baby yet. And also if my dad's back. Your mom should probably call my mom and explain everything."

I pull Abby's card out of my pocket. "Don't worry. I know your number."

"You keep my card in your pocket?"

"Where else would I keep it?"

Abby takes the card and rubs her fingers over it. It's all bent and curved from being pushed up against Superman every day. "I can give you a new one when we get back to the room if you want."

"Nah." I take the card and put it back in my pocket, right next to Superman. "I like it just like this."

Perfect Day

I STEP OUT OF THE CAR AND STAND OUTSIDE THE SCHOOL BUILD-ing watching the trees. No leaves move. Not even one. Finally, after a week of waiting, it's perfectly still.

Abby probably noticed how still it is, too. Of course she noticed. We've been waiting for this day to finally get here, and now it is.

She's probably almost as excited as me.

But she's not in the classroom.

The bell rings. She's still not here.

Maybe she's just running late. Or maybe she missed the bus and her mom will bring her to school any minute. Can people drive a car with a baby inside them?

After we finish reading and Abby still isn't here, I run up to

Mrs. Raines's desk. "I think something's wrong."

"What is it?"

"Did you know that Abby isn't here?"

"Yes, Lester. I did notice that when I took attendance earlier this morning," Mrs. Raines says.

"Why is she gone?"

Mrs. Raines shrugs. "I would assume it's because she's sick. That's why most students miss school."

"But she can't be sick today! We're supposed to do my science experiment after school."

"I don't think germs care much about your science experiment, Lester."

There are twenty-six other kids in this classroom, twenty-six kids who could have gotten germs and been sick today, and it wouldn't have ruined my experiment at all. But they're all here. Every single one of them.

All through the morning, I keep checking the door every few minutes, just in case she feels better and decides to come to school. That can happen with being sick. One time I threw up in the morning and felt completely better by lunch.

But lunch comes and Abby still isn't here.

After lunch, I walk out the recess doors by myself. The sun is shining. The air around me is completely still. It's the absolute most perfect day for doing my science experiment.

Why can't she be here?

I grab Superman out of my pocket and fly him all the way to the swings. Then I fly him around while I'm swinging, which usually makes me feel better. But it doesn't because I know that none of this is going to make Abby get well so we can do my experiment tonight.

Stupid Superman. Even you can't fix this. I throw him as hard as I can into the big open grassy area that was empty a second ago but now . . . Ricky? There he is, leaning over to pick up a kickball. And Superman is flying straight toward him.

"Ricky! Watch out!"

He stands up and looks toward me right as Superman slams him between the eyes.

I drag my feet in the mulch until I've slowed down enough to jump off the swings. Then I run to get Superman as fast as I can. But when I get there, Ricky's already holding him.

"Did you just throw this at me?" Ricky asks. There's a red mark between his eyes.

"No." I grab for Superman, but Ricky holds him way up in the air over his head.

"No? Then why did this piece of plastic just hit me?"

"I threw him and this is just where he landed. I didn't mean to hit you."

"Ricky!" Connor yells from the field. "If you don't get back here, you're benched for the rest of recess."

"You can't bench me. I'm a captain."

Connor turns around and walks into the middle of a group

of kids. "Anyone else want to be captain?" A bunch of kids raise their hands.

"I'm coming," Ricky yells toward the field, then turns back to me. "You didn't mean to hit me? Well, I didn't mean to throw your stupid toy over the fence." He swings his arm back and hurls Superman into the air. "No wait. I did."

Superman soars over the grass and above the swings and lands on the other side of the fence where we're not allowed to go. His red boots are sticking up out of the tall grass. He's not very far away from the fence, maybe even close enough to reach.

My arm fits through the chain links up to my elbow, but that's as far as it will go. Superman is still about a foot away.

I pull my arm back and feel a scrape run down the inside of my entire arm—all the way from my elbow to my wrist. There's blood and stinging and—

"Ooooooooowwwwww! Mrs. Raines!" I yell in my *emergency* voice and run across the playground to find her.

"Oh, good grief, Lester. How in the world did you manage to do that?"

The blood is oozing out now. It's more blood than I've seen in my whole life, and it's coming out of me!

"Here." Mrs. Raines takes my arm and puts it up against my chest. "Hold your arm like this on your way to the nurse so the cut is covered. Can you do that?"

"I don't know where the nurse's room is!"

"Just go to the main office. I'll call so they know you're coming."

When I turn down the second hallway, Mr. Marmel is walking toward me. He leads me through the office and down the back hallway to a room with these pink bed-looking things that have thin paper laid out on them. They look like the things you sit on at the doctor's office, but they're lower to the ground.

I sit down on one of them.

Mr. Marmel sits down facing me and puts on a pair of gloves. He tries to take my hand and pull it away from my chest, but I hold it even tighter to my body.

"Lester, I can't fix it up if you don't let me see it."

"You're not the nurse."

"She got sick and had to go home, which means you're stuck with me." He smiles and tries to pull my arm down again.

"It's going to sting!"

"It might sting a little, Lester, but once we clean it up and get a bandage on it, it'll feel better. I promise."

Slowly, I let him pull my arm away from my chest.

"That's not so bad," he says.

"Really?"

"It's barely more than a scrape." He takes me over to the sink and cleans it off. "So, why don't you tell me how this happened?"

I tell Mr. Marmel about Ricky throwing Superman over the fence and how I cut myself trying to save him. I wait for

Mr. Marmel to say how this is all Ricky's fault and how Ricky's in trouble now, but he doesn't. He just tells me to sit down.

"Can we go get Superman?"

He takes a first aid kit out of one of the cabinets and squeezes some gooey stuff on my scrape. Then he cuts a piece of white cotton from a roll and tapes it to my arm.

"Please?"

"I have a meeting soon, and you need to get back to class."

"It won't take long. I remember right where he is."

He opens another cabinet and pulls out a new shirt for me to wear since mine is covered in blood.

"I know Superman is important to you," he says, after I change, "but I just can't rearrange my schedule for a toy."

"He's not a toy."

"Lester . . ."

"He's not! I mean, I used to play with him a long time ago when Dad first gave him to me. I would fly Superman around and Dad would fly me around and we would save things together. But now . . . he just goes in my pocket."

Mr. Marmel looks up at the clock.

"He's out there all by himself. What if someone takes him? Or something happens to him?"

"What could possibly happen? He's on the other side of the fence."

"But I need him." I don't mean to cry, but I can feel the tears in the corners of my eyes.

"I'm sure when your mom picks you up, she can take you out—"

Something green roars past the window.

"It's Tuesday." Mr. Marmel stands up. "Come on. We have to hurry."

"Why?"

"Tuesday's when they mow the grass."

The Mower

I FOLLOW MR. MARMEL OUT OF THE OFFICE AND DOWN A BACK hallway to the cafeteria then down another hallway and through a big black door. When we get outside, the mower is already speeding along the fence on the edge of the playground.

Right toward Superman.

"Stop!" I yell.

But it doesn't slow down. It keeps on mowing straight along the edge of the fence, right over where Superman is. When the mower gets to the end of the fence, it turns the corner and mows along the other edge.

We run to the right spot, but Superman's not there anymore. I look all around in the grass and along the fence until I spot a bit of red way out in the middle of the grass.

But it's not him. It's just his cape.

And there's a bit of blue.

A leg.

"Lester."

I squeeze my fingers tight around Superman's parts, but they feel wrong. There's just so much missing. I crawl through the grass looking for more of him.

"Let's go back inside."

"I have to find his pieces."

"Lester. You don't."

But I do. I have to. "If I can find all his pieces, I can put him back together again."

Mr. Marmel turns away from me and walks back toward the fence.

"What are you doing?" I ask.

"Helping."

We look together for a long time. Eventually, we find another leg, an arm, and part of another arm. But that's all.

No head. No chest with the red and yellow super *S*.

He's dead. My Superman is dead.

I fall backward onto the ground and stare up into the cloudless, windless sky, but the blue gets blurry and all I can see is a giant green mower speeding along the fence toward Superman and me not being there to save him.

The Opposite of Perfect

THERE'S NO WIND AGAIN, JUST LIKE YESTERDAY. IT'S ANOTHER perfect day for my science experiment. But Abby's still gone. My old Superman is still dead. And the new Superman Mom bought me last night is all wrong.

This day already feels like the opposite of perfect, and it's only nine thirty.

Mrs. Turner, the other fifth-grade teacher, knocks on the door frame.

"Please continue reading *silently*," Mrs. Raines says, and walks toward the door. "I'll be back in just a second."

As soon as she's gone, Ricky walks over to the pencil sharpener, and on his way back to his desk, he stops right beside me.

Why is he stopping here? Why doesn't he just go back to

his desk and read like Mrs. Raines told us to?

"What's wrong, Mouse Boy?" He leans on Abby's desk. "You miss Double-Chin?"

I reach in my pocket and grab on to new Superman. Even though his arms don't bend right and his cape isn't long enough and his super *S* isn't mostly rubbed off, maybe holding on to him will help.

Ricky walks back to his desk, sits down, and makes an awful face.

Superman isn't helping me feel better at all. And I know why. Because this stupid one isn't from Dad.

"It's your fault, Ricky!" I'm across the room before I even know what's happening. "Superman's dead and it's all your fault."

He laughs. "That stupid toy you threw at me yesterday?"

"He's not a toy!" I kick the leg of Ricky's desk. "Everyone needs to stop calling him a toy!"

"Lester." Mrs. Raines is here. "Come with me. Right now."

I kick his desk again. "Superman's destroyed and I'll never get him back and it's all Ricky's fault."

Kick.

Kick.

Kick.

Mrs. Raines grabs my arm, right on the place that got scraped. "Oww!"

"Lester." She lets go of my arm. "I'm sorry."

I turn and run past her and out the door and down the

hallway even though she's yelling at me to come back. I know I'm breaking Rules 1 and 2 and 8. But when it feels like you're on a spaceship that's about to break apart and any second you're not going to be able to breathe anymore, the rules don't matter. You just have to keep yourself alive.

Mr. Marmel walks into the library a few seconds after I get there. I should have gone somewhere else.

Instead of his office, we go to the room across the hall with a big long table and a bunch of chairs around it. "I want you to wait here," he says. "I'll be back in a second."

After walking around the table a few times, I decide to sit in the corner next to the big box of unsorted LEGO bricks. A few minutes later, Mr. Marmel walks in with someone else. I can't see the person's face from here, but I can see his brown, shiny shoes. They look just like my dress shoes but way bigger.

"Lester?" Mr. Marmel says, and walks out the door. "I knew I shouldn't have left him alone."

A man with a bald, shiny head and little round glasses peeks around the table. "He's right here, Fred. On the floor."

"Of course he is." Mr. Marmel walks back in the room and around the table. "This is Mr. Jacobsen, Lester. He's going to be talking with you for a little bit. Okay?"

Mr. Jacobsen is smiling. Mr. Marmel's not.

"Okay."

"I'll be in my office if you need me," Mr. Marmel says, and walks out.

"I'm sure we'll be fine," Mr. Jacobsen says, still smiling. Then he sits down in one of the chairs. He sits there for a long time, like he's waiting for me to say something. But I don't because there's nothing to say. I pick up a blue 2x4 and roll it between my hands.

"Do you like building stuff with LEGO bricks?"

"You said LEGO *bricks*."

"Yes. And I asked you a question."

"I do like building stuff, but I have to sort them first."

"Maybe it's just me, but I think this big table looks like the perfect spot for a sorting operation."

I dump the LEGO bricks on the table and start sorting. Blue to the left. Red to the right. Yellow in the middle. Grass pieces in the box. Red to the right. Gray to the left. Black to the right.

"Can I help, too?" he asks.

"Sure!" With Mr. Jacobsen helping, I'll get done twice as fast.

"Lester," Mr. Jacobsen says once we have about half of them sorted, "can we talk about something? Would that be all right?"

"Can I keep sorting?"

"Yes."

"Then that would be all right."

He smiles at me with that same smile he had when he first walked in. "Mr. Marmel tells me that you run away sometimes."

"Do we have to talk about that? We could talk about what we're going to build when we finish sorting. Or I could tell you about my science fair project."

"I'd love to hear about your project in a little bit. But right now, I really would like to talk about this."

Black to the right. Gray to the left. Grass in the box. Red to the right. Blue to the left.

"Lester?"

"I don't mean to run away. I don't plan for it to happen."

He nods.

"It's just . . ." Red to the right. Yellow in the middle. "Sometimes, inside me, it feels like how it feels in the cafeteria when I'm not wearing my earplugs. Like I can't stand it."

He nods again. "Can you describe what it's like?"

Black to the right. Red to the right. Yellow in the middle. Grass in the box. Grass in the box. Blue to the left. Gray to the left.

"I want to know what it feels like for you."

"Even if it's horrible?"

"Yes, Lester. Even if it's horrible."

Red to the right. Blue to the left.

"Please, Lester? I really want to know."

"Fine! It feels like a crazy mix of chemicals is bubbling up inside me and if I don't do something to make the bubbles stop, they're going to explode and blow me to bits." I pull my knees up to my chest and bury my face in them. "Running away is the only way to make it stop."

Wind

I'M NOT EVEN ALL THE WAY UP TO THE FRONT DOORS OF THE school when I feel the wind blowing through them and down the hallway toward me. It wasn't windy this morning, just like yesterday and the day before, but after recess a huge rainstorm came through, and the wind's been blowing ever since. Not that it matters. Abby's still gone so I can't do my experiment anyway.

"Did anything interesting happen at school today?" Mom asks when I get in the car.

Usually she just asks me how school was. She's never asked me if anything *interesting* happened before.

"Well?" Mom says.

"The heel broke on Mrs. Raines's shoe, and for the rest of

the day whenever she walked she bobbed up and down like a duck in water. That was interesting *and* hilarious."

Mom pulls out of the school parking lot and onto the road that takes us through town, past the library and the diner, and out into the country toward our house.

"Did anything else happen?" Mom asks.

"Actually, yeah. This lady named Ms. Larkin sat in the back of the room all morning and typed stuff on her computer. Then after lunch, she took me to the room across the hall from Mr. Marmel's office, and I spent the rest of the day in there with her."

Mom looks over at me for a second.

"Don't worry. She wasn't a stranger. Mrs. Raines told me to go with her."

Mom nods. "So, what was it like?"

"At first, I thought it was going to be scary, but it wasn't at all. Ms. Larkin told me exactly what we were going to do so I knew what would happen next. Then, at 2:15, I got really worried because I thought I was missing science, but it turned out we were just doing history. And I'd pick Ms. Larkin over history any day. Especially because of what happened at the end."

"What was that?"

"She said it had been so nice to spend the afternoon with me that she gave me a little chocolate bar!"

It starts raining, and Mom turns on the windshield wipers. "So, what exactly did you do with her?"

"For a long time we just talked. She asked me questions, and I answered them. Then we did a bunch of problems."

"What did you talk about?"

"A lot of things."

"Like what?"

"It was mostly just about school and other stuff like that."

"What other stuff?"

"I can't remember now. That was two hours ago."

"What about the problems?" Mom asks. "Do you remember those?"

"I remember that there were different kinds. Some had words in them. And others had numbers, but they weren't like normal math problems. They were more like the kind of problems that make you think."

"Did she say anything at the end?"

"That's when she gave me the chocolate. I already told you that."

"But did she say anything else?"

"No."

"Are you sure?"

"Yes, I'm sure. And why do you care so much about what I did with Ms. Larkin?"

"Because I care about what happens to you, Lester, and I want to talk about it."

"Well, I don't." Not when there are so many more important

things to talk about. Like my science experiment. Or why Abby isn't back at school yet.

I stare out the window at the cornfields. This morning they seemed to glow yellow in the sunlight, but now everything looks gray in the rain, and the stalks are bending over from all the wind.

Mom pulls into the driveway and parks the car so my door is exactly even with the sidewalk, just like she always does. Then she unbuckles her seatbelt and turns toward me. "I want you to feel like you can always talk to me, Lester. About anything."

Rain droplets slam onto our car and streak down our windows until everything around us is a blur.

"Abby was gone again today," I tell Mom.

"Is that what you're worried about? I'm sure she'll be back any day now, and you'll get to do your science fair project really soon."

"But she's been gone for three days, Mom. And I don't know why."

"Her mom did look like she was ready to pop when we saw her a couple of weeks ago."

"What do you mean *pop*?"

"I mean that Abby's mom probably had the baby, and Abby's probably staying home helping out or something."

But *probably* isn't for sure.

"You could call and see," I tell Mom.

"Would that make you feel better?"

"Yes."

Mom pulls her phone out of her purse and dials Abby's number. No one answers.

We call again later in the evening, but they still don't answer.

When Mom tucks me in, she says that I shouldn't worry. She says that Abby will be back at school tomorrow. Probably.

Abby Returns

THE AFTERNOON BELL RINGS, WHICH MEANS THIS WEEK IS finally over and I get two days at home away from school. It's so different without Abby. There's no one to eat lunch with or to swing with or to talk to about my science fair project. I tried to tell Michael Z about my project and he did listen, but other kids kept coming up to him and interrupting me. It seems like he's always talking to somebody and usually that somebody isn't me.

I turn down the hallway toward the front of the school to meet Mom, and I spot a face I haven't seen in four days.

"Abby!"

"I'm back." She smiles her big Abby smile. I almost forgot what it looked like.

"But school's over now. What are you doing here?"

"Picking up homework," says the woman standing beside her. Abby's little sister is standing there, too. The woman smiles and holds her hand out to me. "I'm Abby's grandma."

"This is Lester," Abby says.

"The one you're making the outfit for?" Abby's grandma says to Abby, and blinks one of her eyes.

"Grandma! He wasn't supposed to know until it was done."

"You made something for me?" I ask Abby.

"Well, this seems like the perfect time to take Caroline down to her classroom." Abby's grandma and little sister walk on down the hallway together.

"What did you make?" I ask Abby.

"Nothing yet. I was just working on your superhero chic design. You probably don't even remember it."

"Yes, I do. From that day at lunch. When's it going to be done?"

"I don't know. I can't figure out the cape."

"You were gone for four days, Abby."

"A lot happened, Lester."

"How do you know about what happened?"

She tilts her head to the side. "Because I was there."

"No, you weren't. You weren't there when I lost Superman and cut my arm on the fence." I show her the bandage on my arm. "And you weren't there when Superman got destroyed by the mower and when Ricky called us names again and I got mad and kicked his desk. You weren't there for any of it."

Abby turns around and walks down the hall away from me.

"Abby!"

"I can't believe I spent all that time on superhero chic."

"What?" I run after her. "Abby, wait."

She flips around. "Do you know where I was this week?" Her finger is really close to my face. "Do you?"

"No."

"Of course you don't. You couldn't even listen to me long enough to find out where I was before you got mad at me for not being here." She walks back and forth across the hallway like she can't decide where she wants to stand.

"Abby?"

"What?" Her voice sounds like a barking dog.

"Where were you?"

She stops walking and looks right at me. "I was at the hospital, Lester. With my mom. She got really sick and no one else was there so I had to call an ambulance to come get her." She sits down in the middle of the hallway with her face in her hands.

"We tried to call last night to see where you were, but no one answered."

"That was you? My mom's phone was dead because

Caroline was playing her dumb game on it all day. When we charged it up last night, there were two missed calls. We didn't know it was you."

"You were just gone for so long."

"I spent the whole week in waiting rooms worrying my head off. People kept saying everything would be fine, but I heard the nurse tell someone else that having a baby can be dangerous." Abby looks up at me. "It's all so different this time, Lester. What if something bad happens. What if . . ."

I sit down beside her. "I don't know, Abby."

Abby wipes her eyes with the back of her hand. "I just have to keep my mind on something else. That's why I was working on superhero chic and why I'm here to get my homework. If I can think about that for a while, maybe I can stop thinking about my mom." She wipes her eyes again.

"Lester!" Mom comes around the corner of the hallway and runs over to us. "You didn't come out with the other car riders! I didn't know where you were!" She grabs me in a hug.

"Mom, stop. Abby's mom's in the hospital."

"See, Lester, I told you. Did she have the baby?" Mom asks Abby.

Abby shakes her head no.

"Her mom had to go to the hospital in an ambulance," I tell Mom.

"Who's taking care of you kids now?" Mom asks.

"My grandma. But my dad's supposed to get home from China tomorrow."

Mom puts her arm around Abby's shoulders. "I'm sure everything will be fine."

I look at Abby, Abby looks back at me, and I can tell we're thinking the exact same thing. Mom can't possibly know that everything will be fine.

The Baby

AS SOON AS ABBY WALKS IN THE DOOR ON MONDAY MORNING, I know she has good news. She runs across the room even though there's a rule against running, and Abby never breaks the rules.

"Look." She holds out a picture. "We're calling him Charlie."

His eyes are shut tight like he's sleeping and there's a little bit of black hair on the top of his head. The rest of him is wrapped up in a blanket. "He's so tiny."

"I know. He only weighs six pounds." She takes the picture back and stares at it like it's actually her new baby brother and not just a picture of him.

She keeps it out on her desk all morning. When it's time

for art, Abby puts the picture in her art box and takes it with her.

Abby and I sit down on the stools at our art table in the back of the room. Miss Dimuro, our art teacher, opens her desk drawer and pulls out two apples, three oranges, and a banana. "Artists!" She claps her hands together. "Who can tell me what you see on this table?"

She calls on Tori, the girl who raises her hand every single time a teacher asks a question.

"Fruit," Tori says.

Miss Dimuro makes a sound like a buzzer going off. "Anyone? Anyone?"

No one else raises a hand.

"This, my little Monets and van Goghs and O'Keeffes, is art. Or it will be . . . as soon as you make it." She walks around the room handing out white paper. "So draw. Create. And don't forget what we learned last week about shading. The light source . . ."

"Doesn't move," everyone says together.

By the time I finish drawing the outlines of all the fruit, Abby's almost finished with her whole drawing, even the shading.

"Lester!" She turns to me. "I forgot to tell you. I finally figured out your cape!"

"You did?"

"It's going to be hidden in the hood of a sweatshirt. When

you unzip the bottom of the hood, the cape will fold out."

"So no one would know it was there?"

"Not until you unzip it."

"Abby, that's perfect!"

"I know. And your superhero chic design isn't the only thing I finished this weekend. I also put the finishing touches on the design for my Halloween costume. It's a dress worthy of a fancy gala."

"What's a gala?"

"It's like a gathering of lots of people where the women wear beautiful dresses and men wear suits. They have bubbly things to drink and the waiters bring around fancy little things to eat."

"I went to one of those once."

Abby stops drawing. "Kids don't usually go to galas, Lester."

"Well, I had to wear a suit. And Mom wore a long black dress that went all the way down to the floor."

"Oooh. What kind of material was it made of?"

"Black."

"Not the color. The fabric."

When I remember that night, I don't think about Mom's dress.

"Was it thick and velvety? Or thin and shimmery? Did it have sparkly sequins all over it?"

"It definitely wasn't sparkly. It was more . . . flowy. When

Mom walked, it looked like she was floating."

"What about the sleeves?" Abby grabs a piece of scrap paper from the middle of the table and starts sketching. "On a dress like that, I'd put long sleeves that flare out and look like miniature versions of the dress." She shows me the picture. "Is this what it looked like?"

The picture looks almost exactly how I remember Mom's dress looking.

"Oh, Lester. I hope I can make a dress like that someday." Abby stares out the window then turns back to me. "Wait a minute. How did you get to go to a gala?"

"In Washington, DC, after my dad died. We had to go up there to get Dad's medal."

"What?"

"The night we went to the gala was the night we got the box with Dad's medal in it."

When I can't go to sleep at night, I replay it in my head sometimes. Even though it happened over five years ago, I still remember it really well.

Mom and I got all dressed up at our hotel, then a car picked us up and took us to a place with this really big, fancy room. After waiting for a long time, everyone sat down in the rows of chairs.

A man in a black suit called out Dad's name and asked Mom and me to come up onstage. He shook each of our hands and then handed the black leather box to Mom.

When Mom and I went back to our seats, the lights went down and the man onstage stepped up to the microphone. "Let's have a few moments of silence for these brave men and women who gave their—"

"Mom," I whispered.

"Lester, you can't talk right now."

"Mom," I whispered again, a little louder. "Can I hold it?"

She put her finger up to her mouth. Her head was turned toward the ground like she was trying to memorize the flower pattern on the carpet beneath our feet.

"Please?"

Mom's eyes didn't move, but her arm did.

Now, the leather box was in my hands. With one hand on top and one on the bottom, I pried it open.

There it was. A big silver circle like a large shiny quarter with a ring of gold around it. I knew I shouldn't touch it, but I did anyway. I put my finger right in the middle of the silver circle. And when I took my finger off, it left a print. I looked up at Mom to see if she'd be mad, but she was still staring at the carpet.

I rubbed my finger up the silky purple ribbon to the silver metal strip on top. Under the metal strip was a little pin so you could attach it to someone's chest. But Dad was gone.

There was no one left to pin it onto.

"Lester?" Abby taps my shoulder. Her voice is quiet. "Your dad really died?"

"He was an astronaut. His spaceship broke apart when it was coming back into the atmosphere on one of his missions."

"I didn't know." She leans her elbows on the table and puts her head in her hands.

"It's okay," I tell her, because it is. When someone dies, there's nothing you can do about it.

She turns to me. "How can it be okay, Lester? Don't you miss him so much? I miss my dad when he's away in China. I can't imagine what it would be like if he never came back."

"It happened five years ago, and Mom and I don't talk about him anymore. It kind of feels like he's always been gone."

"But don't you want to talk about him more and remember him?"

"Yes, but my mom doesn't."

Abby shakes her head. "Lester, that isn't right."

If Abby's mom was sad, she'd understand. But her mom isn't sad, because Abby's dad isn't dead.

Thunder cracks. Little droplets of rain splash against the windows.

"No!"

"What's wrong, Lester?" Abby asks. "Is it about your dad?"

"Look outside, Abby. Now I can't do my experiment."

"I couldn't do it today anyway. My grandma's picking me up from school, and we're going straight to the hospital."

"The weather's always wrong. And now you're busy with your new baby."

Miss Dimuro claps her hands. "I'm fairly certain Paul Cézanne was never this loud when creating his still-life masterpieces."

"My dad's home now and my grandma's still here," Abby whispers. "The next time the weather is perfect, I'll help you. I promise."

A Perfect Saturday

WHEN I WAKE UP ON SATURDAY MORNING, THE SUN IS IN MY eyes, which means it's not cloudy and rainy like it has been all week.

I run to my window. The leaves are completely still.

"Mom!"

She's sitting at the kitchen table.

"It's perfect outside!"

"I know."

"We have to do my experiment today!"

"I know."

"We need to call Abby and see if she can come."

"I already did. We're picking her up in an hour."

Abby isn't outside waiting for us like I thought she'd be, so we have to ring the doorbell. Her little sister answers the door.

"He's here!" Caroline yells.

Abby runs across the living room and over to us. "Do you want to meet Charlie?"

"We need to get to the playground."

"Lester!" Mom says. "Of course we want to meet him, Abby."

Mom follows Abby through the living room and into a hallway.

But we need to get to the playground. What if the wind starts blowing or it starts raining and I miss my chance to do the experiment? All so I could see a baby?

Mom walks back to me. "You will come and meet Abby's little brother right now or we're going home and not doing your experiment today. Do you understand?" She's using the voice I'm not allowed to argue with.

I follow Mom and Abby down the hallway and into a room that's really dark. It takes my eyes a minute to adjust, but even after they do, I still can't see very well.

Abby's sitting in a rocking chair on the other side of the room with Charlie in her arms. She holds him really carefully, like he could break at any second.

Mom walks across the room and rubs her finger down one of Charlie's arms. "Isn't he amazing?"

"Well, we think so," Abby's mom says.

But I don't see what's so amazing about him. He's just lying there sleeping.

"How are you doing?" Mom asks Abby's mom.

"Tired, but good," she says. "I get a lot of help from this one." She puts a hand on Abby's shoulder.

"Come on, Lester," Abby says to me. "You can't meet him from all the way over there."

I've never been this close to a baby before. But the sooner I meet him the sooner we can leave here and do my experiment. So, I walk across the room and stand next to Abby.

"Isn't he the cutest thing ever?" Abby whispers up to me.

"I don't know. It's too dark in here to see him."

Abby's mom flips on the light. But as soon as she does, Charlie's face scrunches up, turns red, and he starts making this loud, high-pitched squealing noise. It's even worse than the cafeteria.

I plug my ears with my fingers and run into the living room. But I can still hear him all the way out here. So I run outside.

Mom follows me out the door.

"Why is he doing that, Mom? What's wrong with him?"

"That's just what babies do. Anytime they need something they cry." Mom sits down in one of the white rocking chairs on the porch. "You know, you used to do that too."

"Was I that loud?"

"Nope. You were louder."

I can't imagine ever making a noise that loud. Or being able to stand myself making a noise that loud.

Abby walks out the door. "He's still crying. Maybe we should just go ahead to the playground."

I run down the porch steps, hop in the car, and fasten my seatbelt. After Abby tells her mom we're leaving, Mom and Abby get in the car, too.

It's finally time. No more babies or crying or waiting. In just a few minutes, I'm going to be on top of the curly slide, throwing my airplanes and watching them fly across the playground.

The Experiment

AS SOON AS MOM PULLS INTO A PARKING SPOT BY THE PLAY-ground, I grab my bag of supplies and run over to the curly slide. The closer and closer I get, the taller and taller it seems. I knew it was tall. That's why I picked it as the place to launch my planes. But the other day, I thought it was the wind that made it seem so scary. Today, even though there's no wind, I still feel dizzy when I look up the ladder.

"They let you climb this thing at recess?" Mom asks. "Have you actually been up there?"

"Lots of times," Abby says.

Mom turns to me. "Have *you* been up there?"

"No."

She grabs my hand. "Good. Then let's find a safer spot for your experiment."

"The slide isn't dangerous, Mrs. Musselbaum," Abby says. "You just have to hold on really tight when you're climbing up."

Mom walks over to the equipment in the middle of the playground and stops at the monkey bar platform. "This could work."

It's about three feet off the ground with another shorter step leading up to it.

"It's too low, Mom. The planes won't spend long enough in the air."

"Just come up here and try," she says.

The slide *is* really tall. What if I got all the way up there and felt dizzy? What if I fell off? Maybe Mom's right.

I climb onto the low platform with Mom and open the box of airplanes to inspect them. They're all still perfect—the planes with wide wings and medium wings and thin wings, each made out of one sheet of paper so they each weigh the exact same amount. And three of each type. That way I can measure all three distances, average the results, and get the most accurate measurement possible.

This is it. My first throw. I hold one of the wide-wing planes right in the center of the airplane body. I line my toes up with the edge of the platform, pull my hand back to my shoulder, then I move my arm forward and let go of the plane. It's the exact same motion I practiced dozens of times. But the airplane doesn't fly very far. It lands a few feet in front of me, just like it did when I launched it off the couch at home.

"Try it again," Mom says, and hands me another plane.

I toss it the same way and it lands in the same place. "I'm not high enough."

Mom climbs farther up the equipment onto a wooden bridge. "What about up here? This is higher, and there's a nice railing that you can hold on to."

I climb up to the bridge and throw another wide-wing airplane. It does the same thing it did on the monkey bar platform and lands a few feet in front of me. It was supposed to fly all the way across the playground.

"Let's try up here," Mom says, and walks farther up the equipment.

Abby hands both planes to me through the railing of the bridge. "Maybe it's the airplanes, Lester. Maybe they can't really go that far."

"It's not the planes! They just need more time in the air." I grab the airplanes away from her and put them back in my box.

"Don't get mad at me, Lester. It's not *my* fault you're down here." She looks up at the slide.

She's right. Nowhere else will work. If I want this experiment to be perfect, I have to launch the airplanes from the top of the slide.

The slide isn't dangerous. You just have to hold on really tight when you're climbing up.

I run over, clutch the box of planes between my elbow and my side, grab on to the railings, and climb onto the first step.

Then the second step. Then the third. Then the fourth.

It doesn't even feel high.

Fifth step. Sixth step. Seventh step.

"Lester!" Mom yells from across the playground.

"Keep going," Abby says. "And don't look down."

But as soon as she says that, the only thing I *can* do is look down. My feet are higher up than the top of her head. I'm too high! I grab around one of the steps with both arms.

"I told you not to look down."

"But when you said it, that's all I could think about."

"Just keep climbing," Abby says.

"I don't know how."

"Just let go of the step and move your hands back to the railings."

"Come down," Mom says.

I raise one arm up to get a better grip and my box falls. The planes scatter around in the mulch at the bottom of the ladder. "Are they okay?"

"They're just planes, Lester," Mom says. "They don't matter."

Don't matter?

"All that matters is getting you down here safe on the ground."

She steps to the side and her foot lands less than an inch

away from one of the planes. "Be careful, Mom! I didn't bring extra paper to make more."

I let go of the step like Abby said and grab for the railing, but my hands are sweaty and the railing slips out of my fingers. Before I know what's happening, I'm on the ground in the mulch and my ankle feels twisted around the wrong way.

"Oh, I knew this thing wasn't safe," Mom says. "Where does it hurt?"

"My ankle."

She tears off my shoe and sock. "Oh, it's swelling up. Lester, we have to—"

"Are my planes okay? Did I fall on any of them?"

"Your ankle might be broken. The planes don't matter." She tries to wipe the tears out of my eyes.

"Are my planes okay?"

"They're fine," Abby says. "I got them all back in the box."

Mom looks over at Abby. "Can you help me get him to the car?"

"WE ARE NOT LEAVING UNTIL I GET TO DO MY EXPERIMENT!" I lean forward on my hands and knees and try to push myself onto my feet, but when I put weight on my ankle, I start to fall again. Mom and Abby jump up and help me over to the monkey bar platform. My ankle turns purple, and I can feel my heartbeat in it.

But it doesn't matter. Today is my experiment day, and I'm going to do it. No. Matter. What.

We all sit and stare across the playground, Mom on one side of me, Abby on the other.

"I have an idea for how you could still do the experiment," Abby says.

"Lester isn't climbing anything," Mom says.

"He doesn't have to climb the slide," Abby says. "I've climbed that slide hundreds of times. I've been doing it for years. I could climb up and launch the airplanes, and Lester could observe from down here."

Mom and I say no at the same time.

"After what happened to Lester, I couldn't let you do that," Mom says. "You could fall, too."

"And I have to be the one to launch them, Abby. I know exactly how they need to be thrown for the experiment to be perfect."

Abby jumps up and runs to the slide. She climbs the steps, all the way to the top, then slides down. When she gets to the bottom, she does it again. And again. She goes up and down five times in all before coming back over to us. "See? It's fine."

Hold on to the railings. Don't look down. If Abby can do it, so can I. I stand up. "Oww. Ow. Ow. Ow!" But Abby doesn't have a hurt ankle.

"I can throw them just like you did, Lester," Abby says. "And I'll stand in the exact same place for every throw." She's standing in front of me, holding my box of airplanes. "And you can sit here and make observations in your notebook." She takes an airplane from the box and throws it out in front of her. It lands a few feet away. She throws another one. And another one. She does throw them just like me.

"But it takes two people to use a measuring tape, Abby. If you come down each time, you won't be standing in the exact same place for the next throw."

Abby runs toward the slide. "We can just do all the measuring at the end."

"I never thought of that," I say to Mom.

Mom hands me my lab notebook and a pencil. "You'll be needing this."

When Abby gets to the top of the slide, she stands away from the edge, holds on with one hand, and takes an airplane from the box with the other hand. "This one has wide wings. Are you ready?"

I turn in my lab notebook to the chart I made for my observations of the wide-wing airplanes.

"Okay, Abby," I yell up to her. "I'm ready."

Abby throws the first plane. But instead of going straight, it curves up into the air, then flits back and forth all the way to the ground. It lands a few feet in front of the ladder.

"You threw it wrong, Abby!"

"No, I didn't. That's the same thing it did when you threw it off the bridge," Abby yells back. "I think it's the plane."

The flying pattern was similar. She's right. But that doesn't necessarily mean that the airplane wings are causing it to fly like that. When I threw the planes, I was standing in a completely different part of the playground than Abby is now. For the experiment to work, each plane has to be launched from the exact same place. "Just throw another one," I tell her.

"Wide-wing number two," Abby says, and launches it just like she did before. The plane curves up and flits to the ground. The third one does the same thing.

I record the flight patterns in my chart. If all three wide-wing planes have the same flying pattern and go about the same distance when Abby throws them, then it is the planes.

Wide-wing planes don't go far at all. That means my hypothesis is probably wrong, and one of the other two types of planes will be the one to soar across the playground. But I won't know for sure until Abby finishes throwing all of them. In a science experiment, you can't draw conclusions until the end.

"What do you want me to do?" Abby asks from the top of the slide.

"We still have two wing shapes to test, Abby. Throw another one."

She grabs an airplane out of the box. "Thin-wing number one."

I turn to the thin-wing chart in my notebook.

This time, the plane goes straight like it's going to soar across the playground.

Yes, yes, yes!

Then it takes a nosedive straight down to the ground. The

next one flies a little farther and nosedives. The one after that nosedives almost right away. Even though they went different distances, the flight patterns were the same.

The wide-wings didn't go far. The thin-wings didn't either.

For weeks, each time I imagined this moment, I always saw the planes soaring way across the playground. But it might not happen.

"Ready?" Abby asks. She's holding one of the medium-wing planes.

But I'm not ready. The medium-wing plane might nosedive too. Or it might float around and land next to the ladder like the wide-wing planes.

Mom pats my back. "You won't know until you try, Lester."

I won't know until I try. "All right, Abby. Throw it."

Please go far. Please go far. Please go far.

Abby launches the plane just like the others. It starts out perfectly, then it curves around, soars through the air, and lands in the grass way behind the slide.

"Does that count, Mom? Does going backward count?"

"I don't know. This is your experiment."

My research question didn't say anything about going forward. I was just trying to figure out which wing type made the planes go the farthest. So I guess backward could count. But that's not what it was supposed to do.

"I think there was wind," Abby says.

The leaves aren't moving at all. Neither is Abby's hair.

"Everything is completely still, Abby."

"Now it is, but a second ago, right as I was throwing it, I swear I felt some wind."

"Then that one doesn't count. Throw another one, Abby! Fast, before the wind comes again."

Abby takes another medium-wing plane out of the box and launches it into the air. This time it doesn't curve at all. It glides straight across the playground, past the mulch. IT'S STAYING UP IN THE AIR!!! It finally lands way out in the grass, almost all the way to the kickball field.

"Throw the next one, Abby!"

She picks up the final plane and launches it perfectly, just like she did all the others. It soars across the playground and lands a little to the right of the last one.

"Medium-wing planes win!"

Abby slides down the curly slide and runs over to us. "Sorry, Lester."

"It was the wind's fault, Abby. Not yours."

"No, I'm sorry your hypothesis wasn't right."

"That's okay. In science, hypotheses are wrong all the time. But did you see those medium-wing planes?"

"Of course I did. I'm the one who threw them."

I reach in my supply bag and pull out the measuring tape. "Can you and Mom go measure the distances now? I can't wait to see how far they flew."

Monday

MOM WROTE A NOTE THIS MORNING TELLING MRS. RAINES that I should keep my ankle elevated today. I told her I was fine and that it barely hurt anymore, but she said she wasn't going to take any chances, which means that now my knee hurts, too, from not bending it for the last three hours.

Our classroom door swings open. Mr. Barnes, the man who cleans the bathrooms, slides another desk into the room and puts it right behind mine.

"You using this extra chair, buddy?" he asks.

"Yes, but I don't want to be."

Mr. Barnes laughs. He scoots the chair out from under my leg and puts it next to the desk behind me.

I can finally bend my leg again!

As soon as Mr. Barnes walks out the door, Mr. Marmel and a girl I've never seen before walk into the room. The girl is really tall, almost as tall as Mrs. Raines, and her hair is black with these tight little curls that spring out from her head in all directions.

Mrs. Raines walks to the front of the room. "Class, there's someone I'd like you to meet. Her name is Mona Anderson, and she's new to our school. She just moved here from—"

"St. Bernadette School for Girls. It's in Chicago." Mona walks up to the front of the room. "We moved here because my mom is running the new performing arts center in Indianapolis. I'm sure you've all heard of it."

No one says anything.

"Oh. Well, here are some things you need to know about me. I really am ten. I'm just tall for my age because my dad is really tall. He used to play for the Chicago Bulls."

The kids ooh and ahh. Ricky leans so far over his desk toward her that he falls out of his seat. She just keeps talking.

"I'm also tall because I love wearing shoes with heels." She kicks her foot back behind her. Her bright green sandals sort of look like flip-flops but have little heels on the backs of them. She must be really good at balancing, or else she'd fall over walking in those.

"Thank you for that great introduction, Mona." Mrs. Raines smiles at her. "You'll be sitting back there behind Lester."

"But I'm not finished yet. I was saving the best for last. May I please continue?"

Mrs. Raines looks up at the clock. "I suppose that would be all right."

"My favorite thing in the whole world is art. I won the Illinois Young Artist of the Year Award last spring. That means that my drawing was chosen as one of the best in the state, and I got to go to an art camp at the Art Institute of Chicago last summer." Mona looks around the room. "Now, are there any questions?"

Ricky raises his hand. "What position did your dad play?"

"Center."

"Does he play for the Indiana Pacers now?" Ricky asks without raising his hand.

"He retired from basketball when I was eight," Mona says. "Now he just plays for fun. That's why we're having a court put in behind our house."

Tons of kids have their hands up. Mona points at Connor.

"What does your dad do now?"

She looks around the room. "Does anyone have a question about *me*?" All the hands go down except for Abby's.

"Mona, you can answer Abby's question later on. We're late for art. Class, please grab your art boxes and line up. And actually"—she looks around the room—"Abby, can you come here for a second?"

The rest of the class lines up, except for Mona and Abby, who are in the front of the room with Mrs. Raines. I wait by my desk for Abby since we always walk next to each other in line.

"Abby, would you be willing to be Mona's new student buddy?" Mrs. Raines asks.

"Sure!" Abby says.

"I just thought since you both like art so much, you two might hit it off. Lester, please get in line." Mrs. Raines walks out the door and the class follows her.

"You like art?" Mona asks Abby.

"I'm a fashion designer," Abby says. She pulls out one of her sparkly pink cards from a folder in her desk and hands it to Mona.

Mona looks at the card for a few seconds. "Impressive."

"I have my sketchbook with me," Abby says. "I could show you some of my designs later."

"Is anyone else in this class as serious about art as you?"

"No one."

"Then congratulations on being my new best friend. Now, let's go to art." Mona links her arm through Abby's, and they walk together out of the room.

And even though there's a rule about walking single file in the hallway, they walk double file, all the way to art.

Art

WHEN WE GET TO THE ART ROOM, EVERYONE SITS DOWN EXCEPT for Mona, who walks straight up to Miss Dimuro. They talk and laugh and smile.

"She liked my business card," Abby whispers to me.

"So did I, Abby." I reach in my pocket to show her that I still have her card, but she's not even looking at me.

"Did you hear about the art award she won, Lester? She got to go to art camp at a museum!"

Miss Dimuro looks around the room. "Is there a place you'd like to sit, dear?"

Mona points to our table. "Abby's my new student buddy and we both like art so much, maybe I should sit next to her."

"Great idea," Miss Dimuro says. "Lester, come here."

As I walk up to her desk, Mona walks to the back of the room and sits down in my seat.

"You can sit next to Michael Z," Miss Dimuro says, and points to the empty spot at the table on the opposite side of the room from Abby.

I sit beside Michael Z in Mrs. Raines's class and he's always nice to me. But the empty seat is also across the table from Ricky.

"Abby's my friend, Miss Dimuro. I always sit with her!"

"Lester, dear, we're all friends here." Miss Dimuro looks up at the class and laughs. "Did you hear that? I just made a rhyme. I'm a poet who doesn't know it." She laughs again and walks over to her desk, leaving me standing up in front of the class all alone.

Mona holds my art box in the air. "Um . . . there's an art box here that says *Mussel-BUM* on it." She says *BUM* louder than the rest of my name.

The whole class laughs.

"It's *BAUM* with an *ow* like what you say when you get hurt. Mussel-*BAUM*." I run back and grab my art box away from Mona.

"This is my seat," I say to Abby. "Tell Miss Dimuro that you want me to sit here."

"She's the teacher, Lester. You have to do what she says."

It's true. *Rule 2: Do what my teacher says to do when she says to do it.*

"Lester, dear, the art is waiting to be made," Miss Dimuro says. "Please sit down now."

"Go," whispers Abby.

Michael Z smiles at me. He's always nice. Maybe it won't be so bad. Maybe Ricky will be nice to me, too. Actually, he hasn't been mean to me in a while.

"Hi, Lester," Michael Z says when I get to my new table.

I put my art box down and sit on the stool across the table from Ricky.

"Hi, Mussel-BUM," Ricky whispers.

Nope. Not nice.

"I said, hi, Mussel-BUM."

Across the room, Abby's whispering with Mona. Stupid, seat-stealing Mona.

"Oh, Mussel-BUM."

"Don't call me that!" I whisper back to him.

"Call you what?"

"Mussel-bum," I whisper louder.

"What?"

"Mussel-bum," I say a little louder.

He puts his hand up to his ear. "I can't hear you. What?"

"Mussel-bum!" I yell.

Miss Dimuro runs over to our table. "What in the name of Pablo Picasso is going on here?"

"Ricky keeps calling me Mussel-BUM," I tell her.

"Class, let's put our art lesson on hold and take advantage

of this teachable moment. If there is ever a time when someone is doing something that upsets you, you should always let them know about it so they can stop. Just use an *I feel* statement. Lester will demonstrate for us."

"I will?"

Miss Dimuro nods. "Don't worry. It's easy."

"I really have to do this?"

"Yes. Just say his name and tell him what he's doing that upsets you. Go ahead, Lester dear."

I hate Rule 2.

"Lester?"

I can't look at his face so I stare down at his red art box. "Ricky . . ."

"Now tell him what he's doing," Miss Dimuro says.

"When you call me Mussel-BUM . . ." I say the *bum* part louder like he does.

"Good, Lester. Now say: *I feel* . . . and tell him how it makes you feel."

I glance up at Ricky. He's smiling like this is the funniest joke he's ever heard.

"Come on, Lester. Tell him how you feel."

"Mad."

"You have to say, *I* feel *mad*."

"I feel mad."

"Good, good. Now tell him why."

"Because Mussel-bum is not my name."

"Perfect, Lester. Now Ricky knows he's bothering you, and he can stop." She looks at Ricky. "This takes cooperation from you, too."

"Okay," Ricky says.

Miss Dimuro walks back up to the front of the room. "Life is all about learning how to get along with each other. Even in art class."

"You guys are lucky we got a new art teacher this year," Michael Z says. "If Woodward was still here, you'd both be in Marmel's office right now."

"And we would have taken you with us," Ricky says to Michael Z.

Miss Dimuro puts up a poster filled with a circle of color. "Has anyone ever heard of the color spectrum before? Or any kind of spectrum for that matter?"

Mona puts her hand in the air.

"Mona, dear. Thank you for volunteering."

Mona starts talking, but I can't focus on anything she's saying because all I can hear is Ricky.

"Mussel-bum. Mussel-bum. Mussel-bum."

I grab the bottom of my stool and hold myself tight and try to keep myself from yelling again, but he doesn't stop. He just keeps saying it.

"Mussel-bum. Mussel-bum. Mussel-bum."

Words bubble up to my mouth and force their way out. "Shut up, Ricky! Shut up! Shut up! Shut up!"

Mona

WHEN LUNCH IS OVER, I RUN STRAIGHT TOWARD THE SWINGS like Abby and I always do. I didn't get to talk about my experiment at all during lunch because every time I opened my mouth, Mona was saying something about art museums and art camps and all the art awards she's won. But that's okay because once we're swinging, I can tell Abby all about my conclusion.

But when I get to the swings, Abby isn't there. She's not even running toward me.

I finally find her sitting at a picnic table with Mona up by the building. A bunch of kids are gathered around them.

"No, I will not get you his autograph," Mona says. "If you're here because you want to get to know me, fine. But if you just want to talk about my dad, you can leave."

All the kids run away except for Sydney, the girl who sits in front of Michael Z and always wears her hair in two long braids.

"Um . . . do you play any sports?" asks Sydney.

"I used to play tennis," Mona says.

"Cool," Sydney says, and runs away too.

"You don't want to talk about my dad, do you?" Mona looks at Abby.

"I kind of hate sports," Abby says.

"Good. Once people hear about my dad, that's all they care about. I shouldn't have even told anyone about him playing for the Bulls." Mona looks at me. "What do you want?"

"There are still two empty swings, Abby. If we run, we can probably get them."

Abby doesn't run. She doesn't even look at me.

"Come on! I want to tell you about my conclusion."

"Want me to get the teacher?" Mona asks.

"I'm not swinging today, Lester."

"But we always swing together."

"Mona and I are looking at the design for my Halloween costume." Abby's sketchbook is out on the table and open to the page with the design for her black gala dress.

I sit down on the bench beside her.

"Are you stupid or something?" Mona says. "We don't want you here."

I wait for Abby to tell Mona that I'm not stupid and that she *does* want me here, but Abby doesn't say either of those things. She just tells me to go.

"But we always spend recess together."

"Not today, Lester."

I look right at Abby. "You really want me to go?"

"Yes." She doesn't take her eyes off the drawing.

So I do. I walk away, and I don't mean to listen to them, not exactly, but I can't help it because Mona talks so loud.

"You really spend all your recesses with him?" Mona asks.

"Yeah," Abby says.

"Aren't you worried about what the other kids think? I've only been here half a day, and I can already tell he's a weirdo. All that stuff about his science experiment and how he yelled in art. You must have noticed it."

Abby doesn't say anything.

"Spending a lot of time with someone like him can really ruin your reputation. It can make other *more important* people not want to be your friend."

"He just sits behind me in class," Abby says. "And it's not like I ever asked him to swing with me at recess."

"Then it won't be hard to not be his friend anymore since you're not really friends with him anyway. Just hang out with me at recess. Problem solved." Mona pulls Abby's sketchbook across the table toward her. "Now, tell me about this dress. Are you really going to make it yourself?"

I run over to the swings and sit down. There's an empty one next to me. An empty swing where Abby's supposed to be. Except for the week she was gone, we've spent every recess of the year swinging and talking about science. That's what we do.

Stupid Mona.

Stupid seat-stealing, friend-stealing Mona.

Who am I supposed to talk to about my experiment now?

Science Fair Board

WITH MOST SCIENCE EXPERIMENTS, ONCE YOU FIGURE OUT YOUR conclusion, you're done. But with a science fair project, you have to put your entire experiment up on a board so you can show it to the judges. And if you want to win, you have to make your board just as perfect as your science.

That's why I spent the last four nights at the computer desk in our living room typing up all the different parts of my experiment. I made titles for each section, a big title for the whole board, and I even used this program on our computer to make a graph of the different distances my airplanes flew.

"Lester, you're going to have to do the rest tomorrow," Mom says from the couch. "I have to use the computer now."

"Perfect timing, Mom! I just typed the last word of my

conclusion." I hit Print and the pages start coming out, with no smudges or wrinkles or anything wrong at all. They look perfect, like something a real scientist would make.

And that means it's finally board time!

The science fair board Mom bought me last week has a big section in the center and two smaller sections on the sides that fold up so you can carry it around and no one can see what's inside. But then when you open it up and fold the smaller sections forward a little, the board stands up by itself. The woman at the store said it was specially designed for science fair projects!

I bring the board and my other supplies to the kitchen table and start working. With my ruler, I measure exactly one inch around each of the titles and paragraphs of information. Then I cut them out, glue them on blue construction paper, and cut a one-inch blue border for each one.

Now that every part of the scientific method has its very own frame, they're ready to go on the board.

Since all good experiments start with a question, I glue my research question in the top left corner of the board. Then comes my hypothesis. Then the procedure goes below that. In the top of the center section, I glue the title, then underneath that goes the results, then the graph of the flight distances, and then my conclusion.

All the borders are the same size. All the cuts are straight. All the sections are lined up perfectly.

I stand the board up so I can see exactly what the judges will see. That's when I notice the problem. The right side of the board must have been folded behind the rest when I was gluing everything on, because it's completely white and empty.

The sections need to cover the whole board, which means they need more space between them. I grab one corner of the blue construction paper surrounding my conclusion and try to peel it off, but it starts to tear. The cardboard behind it is all gooey with glue.

"Mom."

She's sitting at the computer with her back to me. She doesn't turn around.

"Mom!" I run into the living room.

"Hold on a sec," she says with a pencil in her mouth. "I just need to finish this sentence."

"But everything's ruined."

"What?"

"We have to hurry. The glue is drying more every second." I grab her arm and pull her into the kitchen.

She looks at the board, then starts shaking her head.

"I know. It's really bad."

"Bad? Lester, this is amazing." She puts her arm around my shoulder. "Everything is cut and spaced so perfectly. I can't believe you did this all by yourself."

"But look." I point to the big white space on the right.

"Then we'll just have to think of something to put there."

"But there's nothing else, Mom. My whole project is already up there, even my graph."

Mom stares at the board. "What about a 'Special Thanks' section? You could give Abby credit for all her help."

"Special thanks isn't part of the scientific method, Mom."

"No, but it would fill up some of this empty space. And it would be a really nice thing to do."

I sit down in one of the chairs. "I don't feel like being nice to Abby when she's not being nice to me."

"Since when is Abby not being nice to you? She spent all of last Saturday helping with your project."

I tell her how Abby is spending all her recesses with stupid Mona instead of swinging with me.

"When did Mona come?" Mom asks.

"Monday."

"But it's Thursday, Lester. Why didn't you tell me sooner?"

"Because there's nothing you can do."

"Sure, there is."

"What, Mom? What could you possibly do? You're not even there."

Mom takes my hand. "We could talk about it. Remember what I told you the other day in the car? You can talk to me about anything."

I pull my hand away. "But talking won't help. Not unless you talk to Abby and tell her to start spending her recesses with me again."

"Lester, Abby gets to decide who she spends her recesses with and what she does. You know that, right?"

"But she picked Mona instead of me, and it doesn't make any sense." Abby and I have so much fun together. Going on the swings. Doing my science project. Talking about science.

Mom sits down on the chair next to me.

I scoot my chair away from her.

She scoots her chair toward me.

I scoot away again.

And she scoots toward me again.

We both keep scooting until her chair is pinning my chair to the sink. She leans around me and tries to look at my face.

"You're smiling, Lester."

"No, I'm not," I say, even though I am.

I know she's just trying to make me feel better. But she can't fix this. Just like she can't fix my ruined science fair board. "We have to go to the store and get a new one, Mom."

She looks at the clock.

It's only 6:18, which is not late at all. If we go now, I'll have time to finish my board before bed.

Mom stares down at the floor and takes a big breath. "I wasn't going to tell you until I was sure, but I can't wait anymore." She looks up at me. "The rumors about Karen are true. She took another job, which means the adult services position at the library is open."

"So?"

Mom smiles really big. "I might get it, Lester."

"What does that have to do with my science fair project?"

"My interview's tomorrow, and I need the rest of the evening to get ready for it."

"But what about my board?"

"You can either try to figure out a way to fix it—"

"It's not fixable, Mom. The glue is completely dry now."

"Then you can wait until tomorrow, and we'll get another one after school."

"But I want to get a board tonight."

She stands up and pushes her chair back over to the table. "Do you know how important the science fair is to you?"

"Yeah. It's the most important thing in the whole world."

"Well, that's how important this job is to me." She walks into the living room and sits down at the computer.

"Mom!"

"I need to work now."

Why didn't I see that stupid other side? Then I wouldn't have to wait until later to finish it and everything would be perfect right now.

I run across the kitchen and punch the board. It flies off the table and lands project-side down. All I can see now is the back of the board with the directions and example pictures. That's where I got the idea for putting blue frames around everything. On another one of the examples, the entire right side of the board is covered with pictures of the experiment. I don't have any pictures because Mom didn't take any that day, but I do have something that could go over there, something really, really important.

I run into my room, grab three planes out of the box on my desk, and lay them out on my board in the kitchen. They fit perfectly.

The only problem is that if I glue them on, when I fold the board to take it to school they'll get crunched. I need to be able to take them off and put them back on again. "Mom! Where's the Velcro?"

"You mean that bag of Velcro I bought two years ago that you promised you'd use all the time?"

"Yeah."

She reaches into the back of the bottom desk drawer and pulls it out. "I don't think it's opened yet."

I cut the bag open with my scissors and pick out three pieces of Velcro. They're big enough to hold the planes up, but small enough so no one will know that they're there. I stick each plane on the board in the exact right spot. It looks like I planned to put them there the whole time.

The science is perfect. And now the board is perfect, too.

I'm definitely going to win.

The Science Fair

EVERY NIGHT LEADING UP TO THE SCIENCE FAIR, MOM PRETENDS she's a science fair judge, and I tell her about my project over and over again until I have every word on my board memorized. By the day of the science fair, I'm more ready than anyone's ever been before in the history of science fairs.

"Everyone grab a book to read, and line up," Mrs. Raines says.

The books are so we'll have something to do while we're waiting for our turn to be judged. But I don't need something else to do. I'm going to be thinking about my project the whole time.

Mrs. Raines walks out the door, and we all follow her to the gym.

Last night, when Mom and I brought my project to school and set it up, all the kids stood next to their projects while the parents walked around and asked questions. But none of those questions really counted because the parents aren't actually judging the projects.

As soon as we walk through the gym doors, I see the real judges. They're lined up across the front of the gym holding clipboards. Some of them are wearing suits, some of them are wearing dresses, and one lady with really frizzy hair is wearing a bright orange lab coat, which is weird because she's not going to be doing any experiments today. She's just judging them.

"Welcome to the seventeenth annual Quarry Elementary School Science Fair," Mr. Marmel says once we're all standing next to our projects. "We are pleased to welcome our judges, all science teachers from Quarry Middle School and Quarry High School. One of these judges will be coming down your aisle and talking to each of you individually. Please wait quietly under your table until it's your turn. Good luck, scientists."

The orange lab coat lady walks toward my row, and Abby stands up. Abby's all the way at the other end of the row, and if her project is judged first, my project's going to be judged last. That means I have plenty of time to check my board and make sure everything is just right.

But it's not. One of the airplanes is lying on the table.

I stick it back up on the board, but it falls down again. The Velcro on my airplane is still there, but the Velcro piece on the board is missing. I search the table and the floor, but I can't find it anywhere.

Mrs. Raines is standing against the back wall of the gym talking to Mrs. Turner, the other fifth-grade teacher. I raise my hand and try to get Mrs. Raines's attention, but she doesn't see me.

The judge finishes up with Abby and moves on to Michael H. Only eight more kids to go.

"Mrs. Raines," I yell. My voice echoes through the gym.

She runs over to me.

"I need a piece of Velcro."

"What?"

"About an inch long."

"When you yelled, I thought something was really wrong, Lester."

"Something *is* really wrong." I show her my airplane. "It's supposed to go up here on my board."

"Lester, I don't have any Velcro."

"I could use tape."

"I don't have tape either."

"Yes, you do. It's on your desk. I know exactly where it is."

The judge moves on to the next project. Seven more kids to go.

"Please. I have to hurry."

She looks down the aisle. "I already told two other kids they couldn't go back to the room. I can't let you go either. Just sit down and wait. I'm sure everything will be fine."

"But my airplane—"

"No, Lester." She walks back to Mrs. Turner.

I sit down under the table. Now everything is ruined because of a stupid piece of Velcro. I should have used tape or glue or superglue. It never would have come off then.

"I think Raines is right," Michael Z says. His project is next to mine, which means we are sitting under the same table. "The judge probably won't care about your airplane, Lester. What they care most about is how you answer the questions."

"Really?"

"Yup."

"What kind of questions do you think she'll ask?"

"You know, all the standard stuff. How you thought of the idea. How you came up with the hypothesis. How you carried out the steps of your procedure. That one's to make sure *you* actually did the experiment yourself."

"What do you mean *did the experiment yourself?*"

Michael Z tilts his head to the side. "Did *you* do your project or did someone else do it?" He looks down the row. "Every year there's some mom or dad that goes all Einstein on a project and the kid who's supposed to have done it doesn't even know what it's about. The project gets DQed and the kid has to do another project or fail science." He looks back at me. "I know. Pretty brutal, huh?"

"What's DQed?"

"Disqualified. It means they throw out the project."

The judge shakes Connor's hand and moves on down the row. Now she's five kids away.

"I did everything myself, except for throwing the airplanes and measuring the distances."

"Was that a big part of the project?"

"Yes." I look up at Michael Z. "What am I going to do?"

"Just tell her you did it yourself."

"But I didn't."

"Was she there?"

"No."

"Then the only way she'll know is if you tell her."

"But that would be lying."

He shrugs.

"You're not supposed to lie in science. Like if your hypothesis doesn't match your results you don't change it. You just explain what happened in your conclusion."

The judge moves on to the next kid. She's getting closer.

"If you get DQed, does your next project have a chance to win the trophy?" I ask.

"Nope. The new project would just be for a grade. And besides, I think the winner gets the trophy tomorrow."

I did almost all of it myself. I found the idea and folded the planes and created the procedure and took notes and averaged the distances and typed it out and made the graph and glued it all on the board on blue construction paper with perfect one-inch borders.

If I hadn't fallen and hurt my stupid ankle, I would have thrown the planes, too.

I pull new Superman out of my pocket and fly him over my head and around in front of me and down between my feet. That's when I see the piece of Velcro—stuck on the bottom of my shoe!

The problem is my shoes are dirty. Really dirty. They used to be white, but now they're gray and the bottoms are almost black. When I pull the Velcro off, the sticky part is almost black, too. But it might have just enough sticky left to hold it to my board until the judge is done.

Michael Z stands up and shakes the judge's hand. That means I'm next!

I attach this Velcro piece to the one on the airplane and stick it up on my board. But the plane looks crooked. I pull it off and put it back up so it's straight, but it won't stick anymore.

The judge shakes Michael Z's hand and turns to me.

I hold the airplane up to the place on my board where it goes. "You're already standing up." She holds her hand out to me. "I'm Ms. Sanford."

"I'm Lester Musselbaum." I shake her hand with my hand that's not holding the airplane.

She smiles at me. "What's that you're holding?"

"My medium-wing plane."

"Can I see it?"

I hand it to her.

"Looks like there's a bit of grass stain here. Is this one of the actual planes you used in your experiment?"

"Yes."

She smiles and looks at all the sections on my board. She stops when she gets to the bar graph that shows the distances that Mom and Abby measured.

"Why are there three distances for each type of airplane?"

I can answer that question without lying at all. "It's because I had three trials. When all the planes with the same type of wing flew close to the same distance, I knew that it was the wing shape variable that made them fly that far. If I'd only done one trial, I wouldn't have known for sure."

Ms. Sanford writes something on her paper. "We don't see many elementary school science fair projects with multiple trials and averaged results. How did you know how to do that? Did you have a parent help you with it?"

"No, I thought of that part all by myself, too. That's how I always do my science experiments."

"Very impressive, Lester." She looks back at me. "Since we've got this airplane here, I was wondering if you could throw it for me. I'd love to see your technique."

"You want me to throw it right now?"

"Just over there." She points to the empty space in the gym

where Mrs. Raines is standing.

I turn and face that direction. I bring my arm back to my shoulder, then forward about a foot, and then I let go of the plane. It lands about halfway to Mrs. Raines.

"It went farther when I . . . I mean, when the planes are launched from a higher place, they go much farther."

"Oh, I believe you, Lester. This is just so great! Actually, I teach at the middle school and my eighth graders are studying aerodynamics right now. Would it be okay with you if I used your experiment with them?"

"Your class would be doing the exact same experiment I just did?"

"I'd make a few modifications, but it would be mostly the same. Is that okay with you?"

"Sure!"

She smiles at me. "Well, Lester. I only have one more question before I go."

Another question? But she already asked me questions and saw me throw my airplane. And she wants to do my experiment with her students. Isn't that enough?

"I would like to know . . ."

Please don't ask about the throwing.

Please.

Please.

Please.

180

"Why did you choose this particular experiment?"

That's the easiest question of all!

"I love flying, and when I found this experiment I knew I wanted to do it right away. But I had to wait for a whole year because my mom used to be my teacher and she never let me do projects about flying or space because they make her think about my dad and that always makes her really sad. My dad was an astronaut."

"You said your last name is Musselbaum."

"Yes."

"Your dad was Thomas Musselbaum," Ms. Sanford says, and covers her mouth with her hand.

"Thomas *Lester* Musselbaum. I'm named after his middle name. Anyway, my mom finally said I could do a project about flying and that's how I got to do it."

She holds her hand out to me, and I put my hand out to shake it, but she just holds on to it. "I'm really sorry about your dad, Lester. When you get to middle school next year, you come see me, okay? I've been wanting to start a young astronauts' club, and I think you're just the kid to help me with it."

"I've never been in a club before!"

"Well, you'll be perfect for this." She looks at me for five full breaths, then drops my hand and walks toward the front of the gym where all the other judges are standing. But she doesn't stop when she gets to them. She just keeps on walking, right out the gym doors.

"I can't believe you were worried," Michael Z says. "She loved you."

"She did?"

"Of course she did. You said everything right. You're like a pro at talking to science fair judges."

"What's a pro?"

"You know, a professional, someone who's really good at something."

It must be because of all that practicing I did with Mom.

"Think about it, Lester. When our judge goes back and talks to all those other judges, whose project is she going to remember the most? Mine with the expanding balloon on a bottle or yours with the paper airplanes that remind you of your dad?" Michael Z pats my back. "That trophy is totally yours."

Winner

WE PULL INTO THE SCHOOL PARKING LOT REALLY EARLY THE next morning.

"Do you think the trophy will be sitting on my desk when I walk in the door?"

Mom parks the car instead of driving into the drop-off line, like she usually does. "Lester—"

"I know you think I might not win." I get out of the car and walk toward the building. "You've told me that a million times already."

"Lester . . ." She's following me.

"Look, Mom. Michael Z thinks I'm going to win. The judge thought my experiment was so good she wanted to do it with her middle school kids! And . . ." I can't tell Mom about the judge wanting me to be in her young astronauts' club. If I did, Mom would probably never let me go to middle school next year. "I just know I'm going to win, Mom."

"But what if you don't?" She grabs my hand and pulls me over to the bench at the edge of the sidewalk. "How are you going to keep yourself from getting upset? I think we should make a plan."

"I don't need a plan because I'm going to win."

"Lester . . ."

"I am!"

"Okay. Fine. Go ahead."

I jump off the bench and walk toward the building.

She follows me again.

"You don't need to come," I tell her.

"I'm just going to the office."

"Why?" Mom doesn't usually come inside the school unless I get in trouble and Mr. Marmel has to call her, but that hasn't happened since last Tuesday during history when Ricky and Connor were being mean to me.

"It's nothing you need to worry about, Lester. Just go ahead to your classroom."

I know nothing bad happened because I followed all the rules. Every one of them. So, if it's not something bad . . . it has to be something good. Maybe they want Mom to be here when I get my trophy. That has to be it!

I walk as fast as I can through the empty hallways to my

classroom. But when I get there, there are no trophies, not on my desk or on Mrs. Raines's desk or on anyone else's desk either.

Mrs. Raines isn't even here. Miss Dimuro is standing at the front of the room looking at some papers. "Happy Friday, Lester!"

"Why are you here?" I ask her. "Friday isn't an art day. And we always have art in your room."

"Mrs. Raines had a meeting this morning and your other sub got sick. I guess that makes me the sub sub." She laughs.

"Do you know anything about the science fair winner?"

Miss Dimuro flips through a folder in front of her. "Nope. Nothing about science fair winners in here. Sorry, Lester."

I sit down at my desk. Who would know when we find out? Mrs. Raines would, but she's not here. Mr. Marmel would too. But he's all the way down in the office, and Mom's in there right now. Who else would know?

Abby!

She would know all about winning the science fair. I run over to her as soon as she walks in the door. "Remember how you won the science fair last year?"

"Yes."

"Well, do you remember *when* you found out that you won?"

"I think it was at the end of the day, during afternoon announcements."

That makes sense. Afternoon announcements are usually when Mr. Marmel tells us the most important bits of information, and this is the most important information there is.

Mona walks into the room, links her arm through Abby's, and they walk over to the coat closet together.

The bell rings. Mr. Marmel's voice fills the room. He tells us exactly what Abby just told me, that we'll find out who won the science fair at the end of the day during afternoon announcements.

The Envelope

"ALL RIGHT." MISS DIMURO CLAPS HER HANDS. "JUST LET ME leave a note for Mrs. Raines about what a wonderful morning we've had, and it will be . . . time for music." And she doesn't just say the words *time for music,* she sings them.

Some of the kids laugh, but she doesn't seem to care, and neither do I because music means it's almost time for lunch which means it's almost time for recess which means it's almost time for math and history and then it will be time for afternoon announcements!

I grab my lunchbox from under my desk and jump in line so fast, I'm in the middle instead of at the end like I usually am. Miss Dimuro leads us out of the room.

Right before we turn down the hallway where the music

room is, Mrs. Caldwell, the front desk lady, comes rushing around the same corner and almost bumps straight into Miss Dimuro.

They say something to each other, Miss Dimuro points to me, and Mrs. Caldwell walks down to where I'm standing. She's holding a big, yellow envelope that says: *To the Parent(s) of Lester Musselbaum.*

"Come along, musicians," Miss Dimuro says. "Lester will catch up in a second."

The class walks on, leaving me alone with Mrs. Caldwell. "Thank goodness I caught you here," she says. "I don't think my bunions could have handled a trip all the way to your classroom."

"What's in there?" I ask.

She points to the front, where it says *To the Parent(s) of Lester Musselbaum.* "It's not addressed to me, so I didn't read it."

"Did anyone else get an envelope?"

"Do you see me holding any other envelopes?" She hands it to me. "Now please do my feet a favor and put this in your backpack."

It has to be about the science fair. What else could it possibly be? It's probably all the secret stuff that comes when you win a big award like this.

I take the envelope back to the classroom and sit down at my desk. The room is completely empty. So, I unfold the clasp, open the flap, and pull out the packet, just enough to see that the paper is white and says *Quarry Elementary School* in big letters at the top. That's exactly what a science fair award would say because the science fair happened right here at Quarry Elementary!

I pull it out a little more and a little more.

"Lester?"

I shove the papers back in the envelope and set it on my desk.

But it's not a teacher. It's just Abby.

She walks over to her desk and grabs her lunchbox. "What's in the envelope?" Abby picks up the edge and looks at the other side. "Lester, that's for your mom."

"It's just science fair winner stuff."

"I never got an envelope like that."

"You probably did and just forgot about it."

Abby shakes her head no.

"Well, what else could it possibly be? I'm the only one who got one."

"I don't know, Lester." Abby walks to the door. "But I don't think you should look at it."

I open the flap again and pull out the papers a little more.

"By the way . . ." Abby taps her finger against the door frame. "Mona and I are going to be sitting at the other lunch table today."

"Why?"

"We want to sit with the other girls."

Even after Abby stopped swinging with me at recess and talking to me as much, we still sat at the same lunch table.

Miss Dimuro walks into the room smiling. "My two lost kiddos. I found you!"

I turn away from her and slide the papers back in the envelope. Then I stuff the envelope in the first place I can think of where no one would ever look for it. Under my shirt.

"I just forgot my lunchbox," Abby says, and walks into the hallway.

"Abby, wait, I'm coming." I run after her.

"Oh, Lester," Miss Dimuro says, "aren't you forgetting something?"

I run out of the room and pretend not to hear her.

"Lester," she yells down the hallway, but I just keep going. Finally, I make it to music and sit down in my seat on the risers. The envelope is poking into my stomach. I try to adjust it little by little without anyone noticing, but the kids around me are looking so I have to stop moving and just let it poke me.

The door opens. Miss Dimuro motions for me to come over to her.

"It seems you forgot to do something very important in the classroom, Lester," she says when I get out into the hallway. "Do you know what that is?"

Of course I know what it is. I forgot to put the envelope in my backpack. Only I didn't forget. I didn't put it there on purpose.

I grab the bottom of my shirt and untuck it so I can give her the envelope, but right as I do, she pulls my lunchbox out from behind her back. "You forgot to grab your lunchbox, silly!"

That's it? She's just bringing me my lunchbox?

"Dimuro to the rescue!" she says, and hands it to me. "Now go in there and sing your little heart out." She pulls open the door and watches me walk to my seat.

I keep the envelope pressed against my stomach the whole time she's watching.

And all through music.

And all through lunch.

I eat by myself today, but I don't really mind. All I care about right now is what it says in this envelope.

When I get outside, I'll find someplace on the playground far away from everyone else, where no one will see me. Then I'll open it and finally, finally, finally find out that I, Lester Musselbaum, won the science fair!

The Slide

WHEN I GET OUTSIDE FOR RECESS, I RUN STRAIGHT TO THE KIN-
dergarten part of the playground. We're allowed to go there
but no one ever does because the swings are too low and the
equipment is too small to be any fun. I climb onto the platform
that leads to a little yellow tunnel slide. I pull the envelope out
from under my shirt and climb in.

Instead of letting myself fall all the way though, I press my
feet against the top of the tunnel to hold myself in the middle.
This is it. The moment where I find out for 100 percent sure
that I won. I open up the flap and pull out the packet.

*Quarry Elementary School. Individualized Education Pro-
gram.*

It doesn't say science fair anywhere on the page. It just has a bunch of stuff about me like my address and Mom's phone number. Then a bunch of people signed their names. Fred Marmel. Regina Raines. Aaron Jacobsen. Susan Larkin. Lucy Musselbaum.

Mom signed this? And the date next to her name is today's date. When she went to the office this morning, it must have been about this. I flip to the next page.

The words *autism spectrum disorder* are typed onto a line at the top.

I keep reading the papers, trying to find something that makes sense, but I don't understand any of it.

My calf cramps up from holding myself in this bunched-up position for so long. I try to scoot myself back up the slide, but my shirt slips on the plastic and my body slides farther down. My shoes stay right where they are, like they're stuck to the top of the tunnel. I reach out to grab onto something to pull myself back up, but there's nothing to hold on to. My shirt keeps slipping and my back slides farther and farther down into the tunnel until my knees are up against the side of my face, pinning my arms and all the papers to my chest.

"Help!" I yell.

But no one yells back.

"HELP!"

The kids scream and laugh and go on with whatever they're doing. No one even knows I'm here.

I'll just have to wait until recess is over and everyone lines up. We always get quiet before entering the building. If I yell then, I'm sure someone will hear me.

So I wait.

But when the whistle finally blows, it doesn't get quiet, not until the door clicks closed and everyone's inside.

"Help!" My voice echoes off the plastic. Then it's gone.

No one's left on the playground to hear me.

Stuck

YELLOW. THAT'S ALL I CAN SEE. EVERYWHERE, EVERYTHING, IT'S
all yellow.

"Lester!" That's Mrs. Raines's voice. She's looking for me!

"LES-TER!" And there's Mr. Marmel.

"Here! I'm over here!"

Finally, there are footsteps. On the mulch. On the platform. Then an upside-down head pops into the tube above me.
It's Mrs. Raines.

"I leave the class for a few hours and you manage to get
yourself stuck in a slide?" Mrs. Raines says.

"Please, help!"

"I'll get his feet, Regina. You get his shoulders," Mr. Marmel says from the bottom of the slide. Then there are hands

grabbing under my armpits and hands pulling on my feet in the opposite directions. My feet finally come loose, and I slide down and out the end of the slide on top of Mr. Marmel. The yellow envelope and papers fall into Mr. Marmel's lap.

He grabs the papers and shakes the mulch off. "Did you read these?"

"I thought it was about winning the science fair, but it was . . ." I try to think of how to describe it, but I don't know what any of it means.

Mr. Marmel looks up at Mrs. Raines. "Go call his mom and have her come back to school. We'll be inside in a few minutes."

Mrs. Raines turns around and walks toward the building.

"What do those papers mean?"

He puts them back in the envelope and closes the flap. "That's not something I can explain to you, Lester."

"Do you not understand them either?"

"No, I do. There are just certain things that are better explained by a parent than a principal." He stands up. "Let's go wait for your mom inside."

"Does she know I read the packet?"

"I'm pretty sure Mrs. Raines is mentioning that when she calls." He reaches a hand down to me, but I don't take it.

"I think I'd rather stay out here and swing."

He laughs. "Me too, Lester."

"Can we?"

He shakes his head no. "Sometimes, you just have to face the music."

"But I already did that. I had music before lunch."

Mr. Marmel laughs again.

"What's funny about that?"

"Come on. I'll explain it while we're *marching* ourselves inside."

Facing the Music

BEFORE WE EVEN GET TO THE OFFICE, I HEAR MOM YELLING.

"I don't know why you didn't just give the packet to me before I left today."

"We had to finish compiling everything and making copies," a man says. I recognize his voice, but I can't remember from where. "We always send this sort of paperwork home with students," he says. "No one's ever read it before."

"Don't you blame this on him!" Mom is screaming at the man. It's Mr. Jacobsen, the one who sorted LEGO bricks with me.

"Oh, I'm not blaming him," Mr. Jacobsen says. "I was just saying—"

I walk around the corner and face the music right away.

"I'm sorry, Mom. Please don't be mad at me."

Mom turns around and hugs me long and hard just like she used to hug Dad after he got back from his training missions. But her hug feels shaky.

"I thought the packet was about winning the science fair," I tell her. "But it's not. And I don't understand what it means."

"I'm so sorry about all of this, Mrs. Musselbaum," Mr. Marmel says. He hands the envelope to her. "I want you to know that I didn't talk to Lester about what he read. We're leaving that for you to do, just like you asked us to in our meeting this morning."

"This is all your fault," she says to him.

"I take full responsibility for what happened. From now on, we won't be sending home any more packets with Lester. We'll let you know they're here, and you can pick them up."

She grabs my hand. "Come on."

Mr. Jacobsen steps forward. "You could talk here if you want. I'm available this afternoon if you have any questions or need help explaining things."

"We'll be talking at home," Mom says.

We turn to walk out the door, and as we do I notice the clock. It's already 2:06, which means it's less than an hour until the afternoon announcements.

"I can't go home yet." I pull my hand away from Mom. "I need to be in class at the end of the day so I can find out about the science fair."

Mom shakes her head, and looks over at Mr. Marmel. "I'm sorry. My son apparently thinks he has won the science fair. Will you please tell him that he didn't so we can leave and I can deal with *that*, too?"

"You don't think I won?"

"Lester . . ."

"I know you said there was a chance I wouldn't win, but you really think I didn't?"

"There are so many students and so many projects. I'm sure a lot of them are really good."

I can't believe it.

"I might be able to help with this," Mr. Marmel says. He turns and walks down the hallway into his office then comes out holding something behind his back.

"What do you have?" I ask him.

Mr. Marmel is smiling the biggest smile I've ever seen on his face. "What do you think it is?"

"The science fair trophy!"

He smiles even bigger. "Would you like to see it?"

"YES!!"

He pulls the trophy out from behind his back. It looks just like Abby's except it's even shinier and the little gold plate on the bottom says: *Lester Musselbaum, Quarry Elementary Junior Scientist.*

"That's my name. And if my name is on it, it has to be mine,

200

which means that I won the science fair, right?" I jump up and down and up and down. It feels like fireworks are going off inside my body.

"Yes, Lester. You won."

"I WON! I WON! I WON!" My voice is so loud they can probably hear it in every room in the school but I don't even care because . . . "I WON!!!!"

"Lester." Mr. Marmel puts a hand on my shoulder. "Would you like to hold it?"

"YES!!!!! I want to hold my trophy more than anything else in the whole world!!!!!"

I stop jumping because you can't jump when you're about to be holding something this precious. Mr. Marmel puts it in my hands. The trophy. *My* trophy. I pull it into me and lay it in my left arm, like Abby did when she held her new little brother. It's perfect. The golden science kid is holding a telescope like he's searching the sky for a new star. And he's standing on a big wooden base that has a gold plate on it. *Lester Musselbaum. Quarry Elementary Junior Scientist.* I run my finger over the words. The letters aren't just printed, they're carved into the metal. I can feel my name, right there, in gold.

I turn to Mom. She's crying. "I'm so . . . Lester, I'm just so proud of you. And I'm sorry."

"It's okay, Mom. I won."

"You did. You really did." She wipes her eyes.

"Thank you for this," she says to Mr. Marmel.

"Oh, don't thank me. He won that trophy all by himself. I think the judges' exact words were 'best project we've seen in years' or something like that."

"Can I go show it to my class now?" I ask Mr. Marmel.

"Lester, we have to go home."

"But I want everyone to see it." I want Abby to see it.

Mom holds on to my shoulders and pulls me in so I'm just inches away from her face, which means I have to do whatever she says. "Lester, we're going home now."

And that's exactly what we do.

The Packet

WHEN WE GET HOME, I FOLLOW MOM STRAIGHT INTO HER
room. "You have to tell me what it means."

She pulls me over to her bed, and we sit down. "You weren't
supposed to read that packet."

"But I did, Mom."

"I know." She stares down at the yellow envelope in her
hands.

"What's *autism spectrum disorder*?"

She grabs something out of the drawer in her nightstand,
walks over to her closet, and unlocks it, right in front of me.

At our old house in Florida, Mom and Dad had a big closet.
It was the perfect spot for hiding from Dad when we played
hide-and-seek. But when we moved, Mom started locking her

closet. I've never even seen inside before. But I can now.

There's a shelf on top with a bunch of boxes on it, and a metal filing cabinet on the right against the wall. Mom's long dresses are hanging on a rod under the shelf, and underneath her dresses sits a black trunk that says *Lester Musselbaum* in big white letters on the side.

Why would she have a trunk in her closet with my name on it? And why wouldn't I know about it?

Mom opens the top drawer of the filing cabinet, and right as she does, her phone rings. She pulls it out of her pocket, which is weird because she always keeps it in her purse.

"This is Lucy," she says. "Yes, I'm sorry for running out of there so fast this afternoon, but my son . . . yes . . . okay . . ." Whoever called her must be talking a lot because Mom's quiet for a long time. She leans against her closet door, facing away from me, while she listens. "Thank you so much," she says finally, and hangs up.

"Who was that?"

She puts the packet in the top drawer of the filing cabinet and closes the closet door. "I got it, Lester."

"Got what?"

"The job." She turns around. "I knew I was supposed to find out today, but with the meeting in the morning and then having to leave again this afternoon, I just figured . . . but none of that matters now because I got it." Mom walks over to the bed. "And you won the science fair." She takes the trophy out of my hands and rubs her finger over my name just like I did in the office. "I believe their exact words were 'best project we've seen in years.'"

"I told you I was going to win."

She grabs me in a big hug. "Yes, you did, one hundred twenty-seven times, to be exact."

"I didn't say it that many times."

"Are you sure?"

"No."

We both laugh.

"Lester, I'll tell you about the packet. I promise."

"When?"

"Soon. But tonight we need to celebrate. What about pizza and a movie? We haven't done that in a while."

I tell her I want to eat pizza and watch a movie because I definitely do. But I also want to know what's in that packet. And now I want to know what's inside that trunk with my name on it.

When Mom goes to the kitchen to start making the pizza, I go to my room. I have a science fair trophy now, and I need to find the perfect spot for it.

After trying a bunch of different places, I finally put it in the same spot it was in Abby's room. Right in the middle of my dresser.

"Are you coming, Lester?" Mom yells from the kitchen. "I'll let you put the pepperoni on the pizza."

"Be there in a minute."

I peek around the corner into the kitchen. Mom's got her hands in a bowl of pizza dough. This might be my chance. I run into her room and try to open the closet door.

It's locked.

A Giant Castle

ALL WEEKEND, MOM'S CLOSET STAYS LOCKED, AND WHENEVER I ask Mom about the packet, she finds something else fun for us to do. On Saturday, we get chocolate chip pancakes at the diner, which we haven't done since that day after the meteor shower, and then we come home and watch Superman cartoons. On Sunday, Mom helps me roll my LEGO sorting cabinet out into the kitchen so I can build something giant on the kitchen table. By dinner I've built a castle over three feet tall, but I can't stop wondering about the packet.

When the dishes are done and Mom says she's going in her room for a while, I get an idea. Maybe I don't need to wait for Mom to tell me what the packet means. Maybe I can find out myself.

I sit down at the computer, open up an internet window, type *autism spectrum disorder*, and hit Search. A whole page of links appears.

Mom's door opens.

"Lester, I know you've been waiting all weekend. . . ."

I try to click on the Exit button, but I don't get to it in time. Mom walks around the corner and looks right at the screen.

"What did you read?"

"Nothing."

She clicks the button on the monitor and the screen goes black. "Lester, tell me the truth."

"I didn't read anything, Mom." I stand up. "But I wish I had."

She pulls a folded piece of paper out of her pocket and opens it up. There's stuff written on it in her handwriting. "Come sit down."

"Are you going to tell me?"

"Yes."

"Right now?"

"Yes."

We sit on the couch together.

Mom looks down at the paper, then back up at me. "You know how you have some trouble at school, and things feel really hard sometimes?"

"Like when Mr. Marmel has to call you?"

Mom nods. "This packet is all about what we can do so that will happen less."

"Like what?"

"Well, remember how you used to have trouble in the cafeteria because it was so loud?"

"But now I have my earplugs."

"Right. Those earplugs helped make school better for you, so in the packet, it says that in the cafeteria or other loud places you'll always be allowed to wear them."

"It's a rule?"

"Yes. And there are others, too. You know how much you hate it when things change at the last minute?"

"I can't help that, Mom! When Mrs. Raines says something is supposed to be one way, I get my brain all set on it."

Mom puts her arm around my shoulders. "That's why Mrs. Raines is going to try to tell you sooner anytime the schedule is going to change. That way you'll have more time to change the idea in your head."

"She said she was going to do that?"

"It's a rule, Lester. She has to."

If Mrs. Raines does that, I'll never have to worry about the schedule changing again. On science days, I won't have to be afraid she'll change it to history because if she's going to do that, she has to tell me first. "This is going to be a million times better."

"It sounds good, doesn't it?" Mom says. "And I think this next one may be the best one of all."

"There's more?"

"You know how you sometimes feel like running away?"

"I can't help that either, Mom!"

"That's exactly why this next rule exists. From now on, if you feel like running away, you're going to do something called *taking a break*. You just have to tell Mrs. Raines, and she'll let you go down to Mr. Jacobsen's room until you feel calm again. It'll be just like how it is here when you sit at the foot of your bed and settle down."

That's exactly what I need! A place far away from whatever's making me feel like I'm about to blow up. A place where I can straighten out all the thoughts in my brain. "And I won't get in trouble for going there?"

"Nope. If you need to go, that's what you get to do."

When Mom wouldn't show it to me, the packet seemed like it was going to be so bad, but it's not at all. It's the opposite of bad.

Mom folds the paper and puts it back in her pocket.

"That's it?" I ask.

"That's it."

"But there were so many pages in the packet."

Mom nods. "Most of those pages were just for me and your teachers. That's why you weren't supposed to read it and why you were so confused when you did. Seems like adults need extra words to explain really simple things, doesn't it?"

The packet *was* really confusing, like those three words on the second page. And Mom didn't say anything about those yet. "What about *autism spectrum disorder*, Mom? That doesn't sound like a rule."

Mom leans back into the couch and looks up at the ceiling.

"Is it something really bad?"

She turns to me. "No, Lester. It's not bad. It's just . . ."

"Please explain it to me, Mom. I want to understand."

Mom takes both of my hands in hers. "All right, Lester. But you have to remember that I don't know everything about it. I'm still learning, too."

"Okay! Just hurry up and tell me."

Mom looks up at the ceiling again. "Well, first of all, people just call it autism for short. And as for what it is, it's sort of like . . . a part of you."

"Part of me like my arm?"

"No, it's more like part of your brain. Actually . . . it's more like part of how your brain works."

"My brain?"

"Yeah. You know how loud noise really bothers you? Well, that's one part of it. And how you can't stand it when the schedule changes? That's another part of it."

"Those things are autism?"

"Yes. And how sometimes your brain feels like it's going to explode if you don't run away—that's a part of it, too."

"So, autism is controlling my brain? Like that guy on Superman yesterday whose brain was being controlled by that evil computer?"

Mom laughs, but I don't see what's funny. No one laughed when the evil computer brain guy destroyed half of Metropolis.

"Nothing's controlling you, Lester. But when someone's brain works like yours does, they call it autism." Mom puts her arm around me. "And now that we know your brain works like this, teachers at your school can do things to help make it easier for you."

"That's why we have the rules?"

"Exactly."

Mom and I sit there on the couch for a while. My brain feels full, like it can't possibly think of anything else.

But then it does.

Tomorrow at school, my new autism rules won't be the only thing that'll be different. I'm not just Lester Musselbaum anymore. I'm Lester Musselbaum, Junior Scientist. And when I walk in the room tomorrow holding my trophy, everyone's going to know it.

Trophy

I HOLD MY TROPHY WITH THE GOLDEN SCIENCE KID AND NAME-
plate facing outward, just like I practiced last night, and step
into the classroom.

Kids keep walking around. Talking. Putting things away.
Laughing. I stand there and wait for them to notice me.

No one does.

The seat in front of me is empty, which means Abby's not
here yet. I'm sure *she'll* want to see my trophy. Everything will
be okay when Abby gets here.

Michael Z walks in the door and stops beside me. "Told ya
you'd win. I'm pretty much always right about these things."
He taps his fingernail on the golden science kid. "It's not real
gold, but they put your name on it. That's a nice touch." He

walks across the room and sits down in Abby's desk.

I follow him. "What are you doing in Abby's seat?"

"Abby doesn't sit here anymore." He points to the other side of the room. Abby's behind Ricky and in front of Mona. Mona's leaning over her desk, whispering something in Abby's ear.

The bell rings, and Mr. Marmel's voice booms over the loudspeaker. "Good morning, Quarry Elementary School students. The first two weeks of October have just flown by, haven't they? And two weeks from today will mark the beginning of Fall Fun Week."

Who cares about that?

But a lot of kids must care about it because everyone in class starts cheering.

"During Fall Fun Week, each grade level will have their own special activity," Mr. Marmel says.

"Lester," Mrs. Raines whispers in my ear, "please sit down."

"The seats are all messed up."

"It's just a new seating chart, Lester. I make a new one every six weeks or so."

"We have to sit in these same seats for the next six weeks?"

"Not if certain people can't stop talking. Hold on a second." Mrs. Raines looks across the room at Mona and Abby. "Girls!"

They stop talking. Abby turns around and stares down at her desk.

"Do I still sit here?" I ask Mrs. Raines.

"I kept your seat in the exact same place, Lester."

"But everyone else's changed." I sit down in my desk. "And you're supposed to tell me *before* anything changes." That's one of my new autism rules Mom told me about last night.

She kneels down beside my desk. "I'm sorry, but you left school early on Friday. That's when we switched."

"I didn't want to leave!"

"I know."

"And I didn't even get to show everyone my trophy." I scoot it across my desk so she can see it.

She smiles up at me. "Would you like to show it to the class today?"

"Yes! When would I do it?"

"Sometime after announcements."

"Morning or afternoon?"

"Morning. But right now, you need to listen."

I sit up straight and tall and listen just like she says.

"On Friday of Fall Fun Week," Mr. Marmel says over the speaker, "our oldest students will take the spotlight. On Friday afternoon we'll all go outside and watch our two fifth grade classes battle it out on the kickball field in the annual Quarry Kickball Classic!"

My class cheers again, louder than ever, and Ricky cheers the loudest of all.

"Well, that's all from me this morning, students. Have a wonderful Monday."

As soon as the speaker crackles off, Ricky stands up and walks to the front of the room. "I gotta say something."

"And what would this be regarding?" Mrs. Raines asks.

"Huh?" Ricky says.

"What's the topic of this impromptu message of yours?"

"Kickball."

She looks at him like she's deciding something. "I guess that would be all right," she says finally. "You have one minute."

Ricky looks around the room. "We've been waiting for this game for five years," he says. "Turner's class won last year. And the year before that. And the year before that. We have to bring that trophy back to Mrs. Raines's room where it belongs!"

Everyone claps.

"I already brought a trophy back to Mrs. Raines's room," I say when they stop clapping. "I have it right here." I hold my trophy up in the air for everyone to see.

"I'm not talking about some dumb little science trophy," Ricky says, and looks right at me.

"If you're going to be rude," Mrs. Raines says, "this little speech of yours is over."

"But he interrupted me!"

Mrs. Raines doesn't say anything, she just stares at Ricky with her arms crossed.

"Fine." He turns back to the class. "I'm not talking about just *any* trophy. I'm talking about the famous Kickball Cup. The trophy that's been passed between fifth grade classes for the last seventeen years. If we're going to have any chance of winning it back, some of you are gonna need a lot of practice. That's why I'm coaching a training camp during recess."

"Some of us have more important things to do than play kickball," Mona says.

"You don't understand, Mona. We've been waiting for this game since we were in kindergarten."

"He's right!" Michael Z yells from the seat in front of me.

Ricky looks around the room. "So, who's going to win the Quarry Kickball Classic?"

"We are!" the class shouts.

"I can't hear you!" Ricky says.

"We are!" the class shouts again.

How can he not hear them? If they get any louder, I'm going to need earplugs.

"One more time!" Ricky yells.

"We are!" the class screams so loud that I have to stick my fingers in my ears.

Mrs. Raines walks to the front of the room with her hand in the air. "All right. That's about all the yelling my poor old ears can handle this morning."

Ricky sits back down in his seat.

"Thank you, Ricky. I think you might have a future in public speaking. And I do think that trophy would look pretty amazing sitting on my desk." The class cheers again. "Okay. I guess I brought that one on myself." She laughs. "Now, since this seems to be sharing time, I would like to invite another student up to the front of the room." She looks at me. "Ready, Lester?"

I stand up and hold my trophy perfectly in my hand so everyone can read my name when I walk by them.

"This is my science fair trophy," I tell them when I get to the front of the room.

"We know," Ricky says.

"Ricky," Mrs. Raines says, "it would be awfully hard to run your training camp from Mr. Marmel's office. Don't you think?" She walks across the room and sits down on the edge of his desk. "Go ahead, Lester."

I stare down at the floor so I can think, and I tell them about the whole thing. The airplanes and the variables and using the curly slide and the trials and averaging and how the judge is going to use my experiment with her middle school kids and how I got the trophy from Mr. Marmel. I show them all my name and the golden science kid and explain how a trophy with a kid holding a telescope is perfect for me because I love space so much. When I'm all done, I take a deep breath and look up.

A few kids are looking at me like they're supposed to. Tori. Michael Z. Ricky. But everyone else is looking somewhere else. Even Abby. She's turned around whispering with Mona.

Ricky's looking at me and Abby's not? Out of everyone in the room, Abby should care about my project the most because she actually helped me do it. Without Abby, I would have had to launch the planes from somewhere really low, and they wouldn't have flown very far at all. Without Abby, I might not have won.

That must be why she's not looking at me. I didn't do a special thanks section for her!

"Lester, that was a very detailed explanation," Mrs. Raines says. "Thank you for—"

"Wait." I point at Abby with my trophy. "I'd like to thank Abby."

She finally looks up at me. "Lester, what are you doing?"

"Abby came to school with me to help with the measuring part of my experiment, but when I twisted my ankle, she climbed up on the slide for me and threw the planes."

Now all the kids are looking at her instead of me.

"Abby, come up here!" I tell her.

But instead of smiling and coming up to the front of the room, like she's supposed to, she puts her head down on her desk.

"Abby!" I run over to her. "Look, it's just like the trophy on your dresser, except this one has my name on it instead of yours."

"How do you know there's a trophy on her dresser?" Mona asks.

"I saw it there."

"He was at your house?" Mona asks.

Abby lifts up her head. "To get a book. He forgot his at school and came over to borrow mine."

"Don't you want to look at it?" I hold my trophy out to Abby.

But she doesn't look at me or the trophy. It's like she can't even hear me talking. But I know she can. I'm standing right beside her.

"Abby!"

Thoughts spin around my brain. Standing in Abby's room. Holding her trophy. Abby on top of the slide. Watching her throw my planes. Mr. Marmel handing me the trophy. Me thanking Abby in front of the whole class.

Abby ignoring me.

Abby ignoring me.

Abby ignoring me.

I have to get out of here. Quick.

Mrs. Raines follows me out into the hallway. "Do you know where Mr. Jacobsen's room is?"

"No."

"Then stay right here. I'll call him to come get you." She looks down at me. "Just do whatever you can to help yourself calm down while you're waiting."

Mrs. Raines walks back into the classroom.

I sit down on the floor, stare up at the ceiling, and count the dots on one of the tiles. When I get to seventy-nine dots, Mr. Jacobsen comes and takes me to his room.

Mr. Jacobsen

MR. JACOBSEN'S ROOM IS THE SAME SIZE AS MRS. RAINES'S room, but it doesn't look the same at all. Instead of desks, there are rectangular tables everywhere and the whole room is glowing blue.

"My room is ocean-themed, Lester," Mr. Jacobsen says, and makes swimming motions with his arms.

"How'd you make it look blue in here?"

"Oh, just a bit of blue fabric over the lights." He points up at the ceiling. "If I hadn't become a resource teacher, I'm pretty sure I would have been an interior designer."

"I don't know what either of those things are."

"Well, an interior designer is a person who decorates rooms, and a resource teacher is a person who works with kids who need a little extra help in school."

"Kids like me?"

"Yes."

"Because my brain has autism?"

"That's part of it, Lester." Mr. Jacobsen sits down on a table in the front of his room and watches me walk around, but he doesn't tell me to come sit down.

His desk is in the front corner of the room, and next to his desk is a wall of cabinets covered in the same blue fabric as the lights. The table in front of the cabinet has bins of markers and colored pencils on it. If Abby came here, she'd probably like this table best.

But Abby would never come here because I'm here. She won't even look at me when I'm talking to her. Even when I'm being really nice and giving her special thanks.

"Lester, I want to show you something." Mr. Jacobsen stands up and walks to the back corner of the room. I didn't see it before because it's mostly hidden by some bookshelves that are taller than me.

"Welcome to Beanbag Beach," he says.

There are five beanbags. They're all tan and sitting in a circle on a tan carpet. This whole corner is the color of sand and there's a lighted-up plastic palm tree thing in the corner. It really does look like a beach.

I plop down into the farthest back beanbag. It feels just like the ones in the library except those are made out of some sort of slick material and are cold to sit in. This one feels soft and warm.

Mr. Jacobsen leans against one of the bookshelves that separates the beanbags from the rest of the room.

I lay my head back and close my eyes. Then I just breathe. The spot between the two nonfiction bookcases in the library used to be my favorite place in the school. But not anymore.

"Feeling better now?" Mr. Jacobsen asks.

"I don't want to go back yet!"

"Who said anything about going back?"

"But I feel better. And when I feel better I have to go back to my classroom, right?"

"That's how it'll work eventually, Lester. But this is your first time here. I was hoping you'd stay for a while."

"I was hoping the exact same thing."

Mr. Jacobsen and I decide that Beanbag Beach is going to be my special spot for whenever I need to take a break. Then he explains how Mrs. Raines is supposed to tell me when things are going to change and how I can wear my earplugs anytime I need to.

They're the same autism rules Mom and I talked about last night.

"Lester, your mom asked if I'd explain a little bit more about what autism is."

"When did you talk to my mom?"

"She called me this morning. So, if it's okay with you, I'm

going to tell you some more about it."

"It's okay with me."

He sits down in the beanbag across the circle from me. "Lester, I like to think about autism as a way of being in the world."

A way of being in the world. The words roll around in my head, and even though I don't know what they mean exactly, I like the way they feel in my brain.

"You see, Lester, you have your own way of being in the world. Other people have theirs."

"Am I the only one who has autism?"

"Oh, goodness no, Lester. Autism affects lots of kids, but not always in the same exact way. That's why it's called autism *spectrum* disorder. Have you ever heard of the word *spectrum*?"

"I've heard of a color spectrum."

"Well, just like no two colors in the color spectrum are exactly the same, no two people on the autism spectrum are exactly the same either. You know how certain types of noises sound really loud to you?"

"Like in the cafeteria."

"Well, someone else with autism may not be bothered by that noise as much as you or even at all. Some kids are bothered by bright lights instead of loud noise. That's one of the reasons why I covered the lights in here."

"But what do those kids do when they're outside? You can't cover the sun with blue fabric."

"It's really hard on them, just like it is for you when you're in the cafeteria without your earplugs."

I think I'd rather have trouble with noise than with bright light. I like being outside.

"You know, Lester, we all have our own challenges. Even me."

"Do you have autism too?"

"No, but when I was a kid, I had a really hard time with reading. I didn't start reading until I was your age."

I don't remember exactly when I learned to read, but I know it was a long time ago.

Just then, a girl I've never seen before runs into the room and straight over to us. She looks younger than me and her hair is sticking out in all directions like she just got out of bed.

"My spot," she whispers, without looking at me. "I need my spot."

Mr. Jacobsen stands up. "Lester, why don't we finish talking at the front table and let Rheya sit here."

"I need my spot," she whispers again, but still doesn't look at me.

As soon as I'm out of the beanbag, she sits down in it facing the corner and rocks herself back and forth.

The phone on Mr. Jacobsen's desk rings. I wait at the front table for him to finish talking.

"Does that girl have autism?" I ask when he sits down with me.

"Actually, Lester," he says in a really soft voice, "some of the kids who come down here for breaks do have autism. Others don't. Kids come down here for a lot of different reasons."

"That girl rocked herself like I do sometimes when I'm trying to calm myself down."

"I know you read your packet, Lester. But a lot of kids don't get to do that."

Mom didn't want me to. But I did accidentally and now I know this new thing about me and have some new rules that are going to make things at school easier.

"I think it's better to know what's in the packet," I tell Mr. Jacobsen.

"For you, it might be. But not everyone is exactly like you. The spectrum isn't just for autism, Lester. We're all different."

The Color Wheel

"PAINTBRUSHES AT THE READY?" MISS DIMURO ASKS AS SHE SETS jars of red, blue, and yellow paint on our table.

Ricky, Michael Z, and I hold our paintbrushes up like we're ready to dip them in paint, which is what Miss Dimuro means when she says "at the ready."

As soon as she's across the room handing out jars of paint to the other tables, Ricky leans across the table. "I haven't forgotten about this morning, Mussel-BUM."

"What?"

"Look at me. I won the science fair," he says in a really high voice. "You and that stupid—" Ricky stops talking and looks down at the table.

There's a hand on my shoulder. "Look what I fished up

from the bottom of the ocean." Mr. Jacobsen holds my trophy out in front of me.

I must have left it in his room this morning!

"You're welcome," he says, and blinks one eye at me. Then he looks across the table. "Oh, hi, Ricky. I almost didn't see you there."

Ricky doesn't say anything back to him. He sits there like he didn't hear Mr. Jacobsen say his name at all, just like Abby did this morning when I said her name and she didn't answer me.

Mr. Jacobsen walks to the front of the room and talks to Miss Dimuro for a minute. Then he walks out. He doesn't say hi to Connor or Michael Z or any of the other kids he passes.

"I knew it," Ricky says, as soon as Mr. Jacobsen is gone. "I knew it when you were reading that stupid mouse book at the library."

"Knew what?"

"Do you know who Mr. Jacobsen is?" he asks.

"He's the man who just handed me my trophy."

"Yes. But do you know *who* he is?"

"He's the man who just handed me my trophy."

"Mussel-bum, you're proving my point right now! Mr. Jacobsen is the resource teacher."

"I know. He told me that this morning."

"Did he also tell you that you only go to his room if you're stupid?"

"No. He didn't say anything . . ."

Connor and the kids at the next table are watching us now. I lower my voice to a whisper. "He didn't say anything about being stupid."

"Of course he didn't. Teachers don't go around telling kids that they're stupid. I bet he told you we all have our own challenges, right? And he probably told you some dumb story about how he didn't learn to read until fifth grade or something."

How can Ricky possibly know all this? "Were you spying on me?"

"All that stuff Jacobsen said, he was just trying to make you feel better about being stupid. But it didn't work, did it? Because once you know you're stupid, you know it forever."

"Ricky!" Miss Dimuro says. She's standing right behind him.

Ricky drops his paintbrush. The room gets quiet so fast I can actually hear his paintbrush hit the table.

"Get to the office." She points at the door.

"Oh, come on." Ricky turns around to face her. "Can't he just do another one of those *I feel* things?"

"Now!" she yells.

Ricky's gone before her voice stops echoing off the walls.

"Come with me, Lester," she whispers into my ear.

I grab my trophy off the table and follow her into the hallway. As soon as we're around the corner, she leans back against the wall and covers her face with her hands. I sit down on the floor next to her.

"I've never sent a kid to the office before, Lester," she says, and wipes tears out of the corners of her eyes.

Other than Mom, I've never seen another adult cry before. And Mom only cries when she's thinking about Dad.

"I know I should have sent him before now," Miss Dimuro says.

"What are you sad about?"

"Sad?" Miss Dimuro looks down at me. "Oh, Lester, I'm not sad. I'm just overwhelmed."

"Because of Ricky?"

She laughs a little. "I guess you could say that. The thing is, I know kids act like they do for a reason. And I always thought if I could just figure out the reason, I could help them find the goodness inside of themselves."

Finding the goodness in Ricky seems about as possible as finding water on the sun.

"But then kids like you end up getting hurt," Miss Dimuro says. "I'll move his seat, Lester. That way you won't have to sit near him anymore. And you know what he said isn't true, right? You're not stupid."

"I know. If I was stupid, I wouldn't have won the science fair." I hold up my trophy to show her.

The phone rings from inside her classroom. "Oh, that's probably Mr. Marmel calling to see what happened. I think I was supposed to write a note or something." She stands up and walks into the classroom.

Back at my table, I start painting again. Some of the kids look at me, but most of them are just working on their own color wheels.

"Lester," Michael Z whispers. "This Ricky thing. It's bad."

"I know it was bad. But Miss Dimuro is moving his seat to a different table."

"Not *was* bad, Lester. *Is* bad. Present tense."

"What do you mean?"

"Ricky almost never gets caught, Lester. When he does, it makes him really mad."

"So?"

"Who do you think he's going to be mad at? I'll give you a hint. It's not Dimuro. He can't be mad at her because she's a teacher."

I stare across the table at his paintbrush and all the red paint splattered around it. "Me?"

"Exactly."

"But it wasn't my fault! He was the one that said all those things. And Miss Dimuro just walked up behind him. I didn't tell on him or anything."

"Doesn't matter. Look. All I'm saying is be ready, especially when there are no teachers around." Michael Z hops down off his stool and takes his paper over to the drying rack by the windows.

How am I supposed to be ready? What am I even supposed to be ready for? And how does Michael Z know all this?

"Ricky's never mean to you," I say to Michael Z when he sits back down.

"Not now. But he used to be. The first time Ricky and I were in the same class was third grade. That's the year the kids all started growing. Everyone except me. And Ricky started calling me Mini-Mike."

"Why?"

"Because I was shorter than everyone, Lester." He looks up at me.

"But I've never heard him call you that."

"That's because he doesn't anymore. I got him to stop."

"How?"

Michael Z looks at me like he's trying to figure out a really hard math problem. "What I'm about to tell you, Lester, is top secret. And I'm only telling you because . . . well, you really need to know."

"So, tell me already!"

"Not yet. Before I do, I have to make sure that no one else will find out. Because if someone finds out, then Ricky could find out. And if he knows I tricked him into being my friend, I'd be right back to Mini-Mike. Or something even worse. So, first, you have to promise—"

"I promise."

"No, Lester. You have to promise *on something*. Like . . ." Michael Z grabs my science fair trophy and scoots it over so it's right between us on the table. "Promise on your science fair trophy that you'll never tell another person about this conversation. Ever."

"What if I do?"

"Then I get your trophy."

"What if I tell accidentally?"

"On purpose . . . accidentally . . . it doesn't matter. If anyone finds out, I get the trophy."

"Fine. I promise."

"On your science fair trophy."

"I promise *on my science fair trophy* that I'll never tell another person about this conversation."

"Ever."

"Ever. Now tell me."

He leans in even closer so his mouth is right next to my ear. "I found my thing."

"Your thing?"

As soon as I say it, he reaches for my science fair trophy.

"Your thing?" I whisper, this time so quietly I can barely even hear myself say it.

He pulls his hand away from my trophy. "Yes, and if you want Ricky to leave you alone, you have to find yours, too."

"What kind of thing?"

He leans in close to my ear again. "Something you do better than anything else. Something that makes you special."

I don't have to think about it at all. "My thing is science."

"That won't work, Lester."

"But that's what I'm really good at."

"Ricky doesn't care about science. Remember what he said about your trophy this morning?"

"What about Superman, then? I know a lot about Superman."

"Maybe if we were in first grade, Lester. But Superman won't get you respect in fifth. It has to be something Ricky thinks is cool, something that will get Ricky to like you. That's the whole point."

"But I can't think of anything else."

"Do you want to know mine?" Michael Z asks.

"Yes."

"It's my speed. I may be really short, but I'm also really fast, which means I'm great at sports. Ricky almost always chooses me first or second when he picks his team because he wants my speed on his side."

"I'm not very fast."

"Good, because that's my thing. Not yours."

Miss Dimuro clears her throat. "Color wheels to the drying table. Brushes to the sink."

"But what if I never find it?"

"Don't worry. You will. You just have to pay attention." Michael Z stands up and pushes in his stool. "In the meantime, though, you probably shouldn't get too close to Ricky if there's not a teacher around. That could be really, really bad."

Swings

RICKY ISN'T AT LUNCH, WHICH PROBABLY MEANS HE'S STILL IN Mr. Marmel's office. He's not outside for recess either, so I don't have to stay near Mrs. Raines.

When I get to the swings, I sit down like always and start pumping my legs. If everything was like it used to be, Abby would be here, too. She'd probably even be able to help me think of my *thing* right away since she's really good at coming up with ideas.

But Abby's off somewhere with Mona, and she's not talking to me anyway. So I have to sit here and try to figure it out all by myself.

Michael Z said science won't work, and I know he's right. Ricky doesn't care about my trophy at all. And Superman won't work because I'm not in first grade and Ricky's the one who threw him over the fence.

There's just nothing else. Nothing about me that I'm good at or that Ricky would like. Unless . . .

"Michael Z!"

I jump off the swing and run over to the kickball field as fast as I can. He's right on the other side of the fence, standing behind a white pentagon facing away from me.

"Michael Z!" I yell again.

He turns around and looks at me right as Connor throws the ball. It rolls through the dirt right past him and slams into the fence a few feet away from me.

"Last Sunday I built a LEGO castle and it was over three feet tall. I didn't follow any directions, either."

"You're out," Connor says from the middle of the field.

"It was interference!" Michael Z yells back at Connor.

"LEGO creations. That can be my thing!"

Michael Z runs over to the fence. "Shut up about . . . you know what. You promised that you wouldn't tell anyone."

"I didn't."

"Lester, you just yelled it!"

"But what do you think about my LEGO idea?"

"No."

"The castle was over three feet tall."

"No."

"But that's really tall!"

"Lester, Ricky wouldn't care if it was ten feet tall. And you can't just interrupt the game every time you get an idea." He turns around and runs back to the white pentagon. "Throw it again, Connor."

☆

On the way inside after recess, Mrs. Raines stops our line outside of Mrs. Turner's room. She does this sometimes when she needs to talk to Mrs. Turner. A few seconds later, she comes back into the hallway and tells us to go ahead into our own classroom and get ready for math.

"You're not coming?" I ask.

"Just go on with the rest of the class. I'll be there soon."

She's supposed to be with us. What if Ricky's back from Mr. Marmel's office? I peek around the corner.

He's here.

I'm here.

And Mrs. Raines isn't.

I run next door. "Mrs. Raines!" I say her name loud so she can hear me over the rest of the noise in the classroom.

She looks up from the paper she and Mrs. Turner are looking at. "What's wrong, Lester?"

"When are you coming back?"

"In a minute. Just go get your stuff ready for math." She looks back down at the paper and starts talking again.

I peek in the door of our classroom. Ricky's not in his seat anymore. He's in the back of the room talking to Connor. But he's facing away from me so he can't see me. I'm safe here.

"I kicked them all to the fence," Connor says. "It was epic."

"No one's ever done that before, Connor. Not even me."

"That's why I said it was epic." Connor shrugs. "I guess I'm just better than you now."

"Whatever," Ricky says. "I know you're lying."

They stand there for a minute without talking.

"So, who all came?" Ricky asks, finally.

"The normal guys."

"Did any girls show up?"

"Sydney was there," Connor says. "And she wasn't bad either. For a girl."

"What, Connor?" Sydney says from her seat behind mine. "Were you telling Ricky about all those kicks you missed when I was pitching?"

"He missed a lot?" Ricky asks.

"That's just how good of a pitcher I am," Sydney says.

"Or how bad of a kicker Connor is," Ricky says. "I'm the best. And *you* know it." Ricky pokes Connor in the chest right as he says *you*.

There was talking around the room before but not anymore. Everyone's looking at Ricky and Connor.

"Well, at least I wasn't *stupid* enough to get myself sent to the principal's office," Connor says. "Seriously. How dumb do you have to be?"

Ricky reaches out and pushes Connor against his shoulders.

Connor falls backward and hits a chair. The chair slides across the carpet into the air conditioner and makes a really loud metal-hitting-metal sound.

"Owww!" Connor says.

"You're not really hurt," Ricky says. But Connor looks hurt. He's sitting on the floor holding his wrist.

Ricky runs over to him. "Come on, Connor. Get up!"

Mrs. Raines walks around me and into the classroom. "I heard a crash. Is everything—"

"My wrist!" Connor says, and holds his wrist up to his chest.

"He's totally faking," Ricky says. "I didn't even push him that hard."

"You pushed him?" She looks at Ricky. "This really isn't your day, is it?"

Ricky whispers something in her ear.

"I don't care what he said. You push someone down, you go to the office. End of story."

"But . . ."

"End. Of. Story."

I don't know what story she's talking about, but Ricky must because he turns around and walks toward the door. Right toward me.

I step backward out of the classroom and run down the hall a little bit.

Don't see me.

Don't see me.

Don't see me.

But he does. He walks toward me and doesn't stop until his face is right in front of mine. "This is all your fault," he says through his teeth.

"Really, Ricky?" Mrs. Raines walks out the door. "Are you *trying* to make things worse for yourself?"

Finally, he turns away and walks down the hall toward the office.

Ricky pushed Connor down, and he and Connor are friends. What would he have done to me if Mrs. Raines weren't here?

I need to find my thing. Fast. And until then, I need to stay close to Mrs. Raines when Ricky's around.

But Ricky doesn't stay in our room for math. And neither does Michael Z. He goes to Mrs. Turner's room, and Olivia from Mrs. Turner's room sits in his seat.

I stare at the big white *14* on the back of Olivia's shirt. Think, brain. Think. But it's impossible! Ricky just doesn't care about anything I do. If only there was something about me I don't know yet. Like a secret thing I'm good at.

Once, in a book, there was this kid who didn't know he was actually a wizard. He had to live under the steps in his aunt and uncle's house in a tiny closet. . . .

Wait a minute.

In Mom's closet! There's a secret trunk.

And it has my name on it.

The Trunk

LAST WEEK WHEN MOM PUT THE PACKET IN HER CLOSET SHE
opened the drawer of her nightstand first. Probably to get the
key.

But I don't have time to check the drawer because when
Mom finds me in her bedroom, she makes me sit down on her
bed and talk. About school. And the new autism rules. And
how everything's going. All I can think about, though, is that
trunk and all the secrets I'm going to discover about myself.

Maybe even a secret that will trick Ricky into not being
mad at me anymore.

I try again the next night and the night after, but Mom
keeps coming into her room and finding me. Even when she's
in the middle of cooking dinner or doing dishes or reading! It's

like she knows exactly where I am all the time.

But on Thursday, when we get home, Mom doesn't go inside right away. She walks around the corner of the house toward the back flower bed. The flowers are all brown and drooping over.

"They look sad." She leans down and starts pulling some of the dead flowers out of the ground. "I can't stand seeing them like this."

If Mom cleans out the flower beds tonight, she'll be out here for hours. And if she's out here, there's no way she'll find me in her closet. I run for the door.

"Why don't you go grab a rake? You could make a big pile of leaves and jump in it."

"Do I have to?"

"Don't tell me you're too old for jumping in leaves now."

"No. I just have other stuff to do."

She stands up. "Homework stuff?"

"Yes," I tell her. And it's not a lie. I actually do have homework.

Mom goes inside to change into her work clothes, and I put my homework out on the table like I'm about to do it.

"Oh, good. I'm gonna put a lasagna in the oven, and I don't want to burn it again. Can you listen for the oven timer and come tell me when it beeps?"

"When will that be?"

"5:17."

That gives me almost an hour.

As soon as she's back outside, I run into her room and open her nightstand drawer. The key is right there. Just like I thought it would be.

Then her closet door is open, and the trunk is right there in front of me. I push Mom's dresses back toward the wall so they're not in the way when I open it, and that's when I see what's behind them. *Thomas.* In big white letters.

Thomas Lester Musselbaum.

This isn't my trunk. It's Dad's.

One by one, I unhook each latch. Then I open the lid. Right there, in the middle of the trunk, is a space helmet. Dad's space helmet! I lift it up over my head and set it down on my shoulders.

My head is right where Dad's head was. And if he wore this helmet on one of his missions, then my head is inside something that has actually been to space.

"Lester!" Mom yells. The screen door slams. "Have you seen my work gloves?"

I stand up and try to pull the closet door closed, but it won't shut all the way with this helmet on my head.

"Lester?" Her voice is closer.

I slide Mom's clothes out of the way and crouch down under the shelf, but when I lean over, the helmet slips forward and slams into the filing cabinet.

Mom opens the closet door.

"I'll put it back right now and we can close the lid and never look at it again. Okay? I'm sorry, Mom. I'm sorry. I'm sorry. I'm sorry."

She takes the helmet off my head and sits down in the closet doorway. "Even five years later, I still miss him so much." Tears run down her cheeks like they always do when she thinks about Dad. And this time, it really is my fault.

I opened the trunk.

I put on the helmet.

I reminded her of him.

"It's hard for me to think about him, Lester." Mom rubs her hand over the helmet. But she doesn't put it away. She just sits there with it in her lap.

"It's hard for me, too, Mom."

"It's okay to be sad, honey."

"But I'm not."

She looks up at me. "What do you mean, Lester?"

"I can't remember him very well."

Mom looks down at the helmet again.

"I can remember some stuff, the same stuff I keep remembering over and over again. Like when he gave me Superman. Or how he used to fly me around the house. Or how we all used to watch the superstars together. But all the other stuff . . . sometimes it feels like . . ."

"What?" She puts the helmet on the floor and takes my hands in hers. "Lester, I want to know."

"Even if it makes you cry more?"

"Yes."

"But why would you want that?"

"Because it's something you feel, and that's the most important thing of all. Please tell me."

So I do. I open my mouth and say the words even though I know they're going to make her sadder. "Sometimes it feels like he never existed at all."

She's crying even more now. It's just like when we were in our Florida house and the TV flashed from mission control to the bright blue sky and those streaks of light. Mom reaches out and pulls me into her. She holds me tight and rocks me just like that day.

Then she stops. She lets go of me and crawls over to the trunk. There are still tears in her eyes, but she's smiling, too.

"I don't know what your face means."

Mom laughs. "It means I'm about to do something I should have done a long time ago." She looks up at the ceiling and then back down to me. "Lester, there's someone I'd like you to meet."

We kneel in front of the open trunk. She reaches inside and pulls out a black leather folder. "Here, look at this."

I open it. *Purdue University, School of Engineering. Thomas Lester Musselbaum.* The words are printed on creamy white paper. I run my finger across Dad's name. It's not smooth. It's carved into the paper just like my name on my science fair trophy.

"That's his college diploma, Lester. And you see that ribbon?"

It's made out of black-and-yellow fabric and stuck in the corner of the paper.

"That means he graduated at the top of his class. He was really smart, just like you." She reaches into the box and pulls out a thin, green hardback book. "Here's one of his lab notebooks."

I don't know what all the words and symbols mean, but I see a hypothesis and procedure and conclusion. "Dad used the scientific method, too."

Mom reaches back in the box and pulls out a small framed picture of Dad holding me when I was a little baby. This picture used to be on the wall in our house in Florida, but I forgot all about it. Dad's looking down at me and I'm looking up at him, just like the picture Abby showed me of her and Charlie.

"After you were born, Lester, he was the very first person to hold you. He looked down at your face and . . ."

"What, Mom?"

"He looked down at you and said . . ." Mom wipes her eyes. "That even though he'd been all the way to space, he'd never seen anything more amazing than you."

I stare down at Dad staring down at baby me. "Can I put it in my room?"

Mom nods.

I set it on my nightstand so I can look at it every day when

I wake up and every night before I go to bed. I'll never forget what Dad looks like ever again.

When I come back into Mom's room, she's standing in front of her dresser holding a black leather box.

Dad's medal.

She opens her bottom dresser drawer and puts the box inside.

"Let's look at it, Mom."

"I can't."

"But we're looking at all his other stuff."

Mom nods. "I know, honey, but this is just different."

"How?"

"All this other stuff is from his life. But this medal . . . He got it because he died." Mom lies down on her bed and stares up at the ceiling. "Those days after, they were the worst days of my whole life. And the night we got the medal was the worst of the worst. Being away from home. Having to dress up. Seeing all those people. Shaking the president's hand."

"That man was the president?"

Mom laughs. "You didn't know?"

"No."

"I guess I forgot to tell you. Oh, Lester, I was such a mess then. You remember, right? How I cried all the time?"

"Yes." She doesn't need to remind me of that.

"And that night we got the medal, I had to act like I was okay. For you. For the president. For everyone. It was supposed to be this big honor, but all I wanted to do was go home. I don't know how I even made it through that night."

"I do." I sit down on the bed next to Mom. "You let me hold the box."

"I did?"

"When you were staring down at the flowers in the carpet and we were having silence and then all those people got up and talked, I held it the whole time."

She reaches up to my face, tucks my hair behind my ear, and smiles.

We sit there for a while. Mom's not crying anymore.

"Can we look at more of Dad's things, not the medal, but other things?"

Mom sits up. "Sure. Why not?"

I grab the space helmet off the floor and bring it over to the bed. "Tell me about this, Mom. Did he actually wear it in space?"

"He did, but only on his first mission. After that, they changed all the suits and didn't use these helmets anymore. Then somehow, your dad talked someone into letting him keep this one. I still can't believe it."

I can't believe it either. I'm holding something that has flown completely out of the atmosphere into outer space where the moon and sun and other planets are. "I don't think we should put it back in the trunk, Mom."

"Then what should we do with it?"

"Put it on my dresser with my science fair trophy."

"Lester . . ."

I know what she's going to say. That if we leave it out on my dresser, it could get broken. That we should put it back in the trunk to protect it and keep it safe so nothing bad ever happens to it.

"I think that's a great idea," Mom says.

"But Mom . . . wait. What?"

"I can't think of a better place for it."

Helmet

MOM WOULDN'T LET ME BRING THE SPACE HELMET TO SCHOOL today so I can't actually show it to Ricky, but I can tell him about it. I know a space helmet has to do with science and Ricky doesn't like science, but it's not just a space helmet. It's a space helmet that's actually been to space!

I know I'm the only kid in school with one. I'm probably the only kid in the world with one. And once I tell Ricky about it, everything will be fixed. I won't have to stay near Mrs. Raines at recess anymore, and I won't have to know exactly where Ricky is at all times. Everything can go back to normal. Well, as normal as it can be with Abby sitting all the way across the room and not talking to me.

When Ricky finally gets to school, I run over to his desk.

"What, Mussel-bum?"

"I have a space helmet on my dresser."

"The kind that all the weird space aliens wear?" He laughs.

"No, it's a real helmet. The kind *astronauts* wear. And it's actually been to space."

"Okay," he says in a funny voice and nods his head up and down in really big motions.

"Ricky!" Abby says from behind him.

"What, Double-Chin?" he says to Abby, then looks back at me. "Why don't you take that space helmet of yours and go back to your home planet where you belong?"

How could it not work? It's a space helmet THAT'S ACTU-ALLY BEEN TO SPACE!

"Is that really true? About the space helmet?" Michael Z asks when I sit down.

"My dad wore it to space on his very first mission. Last night I found a trunk of his old stuff in my mom's closet and the helmet was in there."

"That's like the coolest thing I've ever heard."

"I know!"

"But why were you telling Ricky?"

"So it could be my thing!"

He shakes his head no.

"But you just said it was the coolest thing you ever heard."

"That's because I kind of care about stuff like that. Look, Lester," Michael Z says, "you're thinking about this all wrong.

251

Don't think about what you're good at or what you have or anything like that. Think about what Ricky likes."

"How would I know what that is?"

"By listening." He points across the room. "He's talking about it right now."

Ricky is trying to convince Mona to come to kickball practice today.

"Oh man, Lester. Think about it." Michael Z's voice gets really quiet. "Imagine if you were really good at kicking and you helped our class win the game. You'd stop being this weird kid he makes fun of and become the kid who helped our class win the trophy."

"You think I'm weird?"

"Well, yeah."

"Why?" I knew Mona thought I was weird. But Michael Z? He's always been so nice to me.

"Well, you talk way too loud. You wear those weird things in your ears at lunch. You talk about science all the time. And sometimes you just get up and run out of the room."

I thought Michael was my friend. I thought he was trying to help me.

"But you've also never once said anything about how short I am."

"I don't care if you're short."

"And I don't care if you're weird. And Ricky won't either if you help us win that game."

"But I've never done sports."

"Don't worry. Kickball is the easiest sport ever. All you have to do is kick a ball when someone rolls it to you." He looks me up and down. "You're kind of tall. I bet you could kick it pretty far."

I think about what it would be like, me out there on the kickball field, someone rolling me the ball like Connor rolled it to Michael Z the other day. But then I'd have to kick it. "I don't think I could do it."

He shrugs. "Then I'm out of ideas."

I am, too. I'm going to be standing with Mrs. Raines at recess for the rest of the year.

Recess

AFTER LUNCH, I WALK STRAIGHT TO THE MIDDLE OF THE PLAY-
ground and stand with Mrs. Raines.

"I've made a decision, Lester," Mrs. Raines says. "It's time
for you to go play."

"What do you mean?"

"Run around. Chase the falling leaves. Swing. Slide. I don't
care what you do, but you have to go."

"I'll just stay here."

"Lester . . ." She puts her hand on my shoulder. "Do you
know why I stand over here by this tree every day?"

"Because it's in the exact center of the playground and you
can see everyone and make sure we're all safe."

"Well, yes. But also because it's quieter here. This is the

only time of the day when someone's not yapping my poor ears off."

"Your ears aren't off."

"Lester?" Abby says from behind me.

Abby? What's she doing over here?

"Oh, Abby. Thank goodness." Mrs. Raines puts her arms around Abby's shoulders. "Why don't you and Lester go on the swings for a while? Didn't you always used to do that together?"

"Abby doesn't swing anymore," I tell Mrs. Raines.

"But don't you miss it, Abby?" Mrs. Raines says. "Wouldn't that be a fun thing to do with Lester again?"

Say yes, Abby!

"Actually, Mona and I are drawing." She points across the playground at the picnic table. "I just wanted to tell Lester something."

Mrs. Raines walks to the other side of the tree. "I'll just be over here resting my ears."

"What is it, Abby?"

Abby turns to me. "Did you really get your dad's space helmet like you told Ricky this morning?"

"It's on my dresser right now."

"Do you think it would fit you?"

"I know it would. I put it on last night."

Abby gets a big smile on her face. "Then I have a design idea for you."

"The superhero chic design?"

"No. This is way better."

"What could be better than a hooded sweatshirt with a cape hidden inside?"

"An astronaut costume with a real space helmet that's actually been to space!"

She's right. That is better. If I wore a helmet and a white suit with gloves and space boots, I'd look just like an astronaut. I'd probably look just like Dad.

And that's why I can't do it. "My mom made me promise never to be an astronaut."

"Seriously?"

"It's too dangerous."

"But this would be a costume. You know, for Halloween? You're not actually going into space."

"I know. I just don't think she'd let me."

"Fine." Abby turns around and walks back to Mona.

"Abby!" I run after her but have to stop because I'm getting too far away from Mrs. Raines.

"Lester, go," Mrs. Raines says when I get back to her.

"But I don't want to."

She folds her arms across her chest. "You can either tell me why you won't leave my side or you can go on the swings. You have exactly ten seconds to make your decision."

I can't tell her why. If I do, that would be breaking my promise to Michael Z and then I'd have to give him my science fair trophy. "Will you come over there with me?" I ask her.

"What in the world are you scared of, Lester?"

How does she know I'm scared of something?

"Is someone being mean to you? Is it Ricky?"

She can't possibly know I'm over here because of Ricky! But she does. Somehow she does. "Okay. I'll go. But can you at least watch and make sure everything's okay?"

"Lester, that is what I do every minute of every recess!"

On my way to the swings, I turn back every few steps to make sure she's still watching me. She is.

No one's on the swings today. All the kids who usually swing are out on the kickball field. I sit down on the swing that's farthest from the field.

There are a lot of kids out there today. Some of them are in the dirt. Others are in the grass. A bunch of other kids are sitting on a bench in a little fenced-in box on the left side of the field. Ricky is standing in the middle of the dirt on a little white rectangle.

He rolls the ball and Connor starts running toward the white pentagon. Connor gets there at the exact same time as the ball and uses his right foot to kick. The ball soars way up into the air over Ricky's head and lands out in the grass. Connor runs toward the white square where Michael Z is standing then goes on to the next square. The kids out in the grass grab the ball and throw it back to Ricky.

Then someone else walks up to the white pentagon and the same thing happens all over again.

After watching for a while, I notice something. Even though Ricky throws the ball in the exact same way each time, the kicks almost never go in the same place.

Tori walks up to the pentagon next. She's the girl who always has her hand raised in class and sometimes sits on the swing next to me at recess. But swinging with Tori isn't as fun as swinging with Abby because . . . she's not Abby.

Ricky throws her the ball. Instead of running to the pentagon like Connor, Tori just stands there to kick. The ball lands in the dirt part of the field right next to Michael Z. He grabs it and steps on the white square.

"Out," Ricky yells.

Tori runs back to the bench.

"Okay, Sydney," Ricky says. "Connor's kick has been the best so far. Think you can outkick him?"

"Don't I always?" Sydney says.

She stands way back behind the pentagon and runs to meet the ball just like Connor did. But she does something different than Connor. She turns her whole body like she's facing Michael Z instead of Ricky. The ball flies over Michael Z's head and doesn't land until it's way out in the grass. It bounces over the head of Michael H, the other Michael, and keeps rolling almost all the way to the back fence.

Sydney runs around the field to each of the white squares then steps on the pentagon where she first kicked the ball. The kids at the side of the field are jumping up and down and cheering.

"And that, Connor," Sydney says, "is what you call a kick."

Michael H runs back to the ball behind him and picks it up, but he doesn't throw it back to Ricky. He drops the ball in front of him and kicks it. The ball flies way up into the air, straight toward me. It bounces in the grass then keeps rolling until it's in the mulch, almost under my feet.

"Mussel-bum!" Ricky yells to me. "Make yourself useful and bring us the ball!"

I'm not going over there.

"Mussel-bum!"

Mrs. Raines isn't looking over here at all like she said she would.

"If you want it, Ricky, you come—" Wait. He can't come over here.

Michael Z runs to the fence. "Lester, kick it back!"

If I kick it, then Ricky won't have to come over here, and I won't have to go over there.

"You're the fastest," Ricky yells at Michael Z. "Just go get the ball since Mussel-bum's not going to do it."

"Hold on," Michael Z yells again. "Lester's going to kick it back."

"No, I'm not."

"*I'll* just go," Ricky says, and starts running toward me.

No! I jump off the swing and pick up the ball. I turn toward Michael Z because the kicks seem to go in whatever way the person was facing. Then I drop the ball and bring my leg forward. The ball hits the toe of my shoe and flies way up into the air, straight toward Michael Z. He takes a couple of steps backward and the ball lands right in his arms.

There. They have the ball back now. They can keep playing and I can keep swinging and everything can go back to the way it was a minute ago.

Michael Z runs toward me with the ball in his arms. What's he doing?

"Michael!" Ricky yells from the field. "You're wasting our time!!" His voice sounds mad, like he might want to push someone again.

"That was awesome, Lester," Michael Z says when he gets to me. "Now kick it to Ricky."

He tries to hand me the ball, but I don't take it.

"Just try it. If your kick is bad, we'll know that first kick was just beginner's luck. But if the next kick is good, too, then you just found your thing."

Me being good at kickball doesn't make any sense. I'm usually good at science and building things and stuff you do mostly sitting down. I'm good at the thinking stuff.

But there seems to be a lot of thinking in kickball, too. I bet if I observed enough kicks and kept track of the data, I could use the scientific method to figure out how to make the very best kick. And if I help our class win the game, Ricky would definitely stop being mean.

"Michael!" Ricky yells from the field. "Bring it back!"

Michael Z holds the ball out to me again, and this time I take it.

I turn so my body is facing the direction I want the ball to go, swing my leg forward, and drop the ball right over my foot. It soars through the air and lands almost exactly where my first kick landed.

"I know talent when I see it," Michael Z says, "and that's exactly what you've got. Kickball is definitely your thing." He grabs the sleeve of my sweatshirt and pulls me toward the field. "*You're* going to be the new kickball star, and *I'm* going to be the one who discovered you."

Ricky's standing at the fence when we get there. "You better have a real good reason for bringing Mussel-BUM onto *my* kickball field."

"You saw his kicks, Ricky. He's good. And that's without any practice."

"I don't care. I don't want him on my field."

I turn around to run back to Mrs. Raines, but Michael Z grabs my sleeve and holds on to me.

"Look Ricky, you know he's going to get to play in the game. If you let him practice with us, he might get even better by then. And think about it—no one would ever expect him to be as good as he is. He could be our secret weapon."

Ricky stares at me. "Fine. But if this is a huge disaster, Michael, it's all your fault."

Mrs. Raines blows the whistle.

Michael Z and I walk toward the school, toward Mrs. Raines and all the other kids in our class.

Toward Ricky.

When we get to the line and I see him standing there, holding that red ball, I think a really, really bad thought.

"What if I do something wrong? What if I'm out there and Ricky is counting on me to make a really good kick and I mess it up?"

Michael Z looks up at me. "But what if you don't?"

Library

AFTER SCHOOL, MOM AND I GO STRAIGHT TO THE LIBRARY. SHE has a cart of books she needs to finish cataloging and I need to start my kickball research.

"Lester!" Miss Jamie says when I walk by the children's reference desk. "I haven't seen you in eons! How's your school library treating you?"

"I like the nonfiction section, but it's really small."

"Nothing like the expansive gem we have here." She raises her hands into the air. "Over fifty thousand materials call this library home so, chances are, if you want it, we've got it. Are you researching something specific today?"

"Kickball."

"That's a big change of topic, Lester."

"I know. There's just this big kickball game at my school in exactly two weeks, and I need to learn the rules and figure out how to make the best kick I possibly can."

She nods. "This is very important research indeed. So, we're looking for some basics and some specifics." Miss Jamie starts typing. "Let's see here. Children's. Sports. Kickball. Here we go. Looks like we're in the 790s, a few rows over from the 500s, where we normally spend most of our time." She jumps out of her chair. "Follow me."

When we get to the end of the 700 row, Miss Jamie pulls three books off the shelf. The first book, *Kickball: Fun for Everyone*, has little cartoon mice playing kickball on the cover. I don't care what's inside. I am not reading a book with cartoon mice on the cover. *Recess Favorites* has a picture of actual kids on the front, but only has a small section on kickball, so I hand that one back, too. But *Kickball: The Rules* is exactly what I need. There are chapters about the field and about the different roles of the people on the field and about different plays you can make. There's even a glossary in the back with definitions for a bunch of kickball-related words.

"Easy peasy lemon squeezy," she says. "Always a pleasure to help my favorite researcher."

"That's it? What about kicking and why certain kicks go farther than others?" I flip through my book. "There's nothing about that in here."

She looks along the shelf. "That seems to be all we have

here . . . unless . . ." She runs back to her computer with her finger in the air. "Lester, my dear, hold on to your hat, we are about to attempt an advanced search!"

"But I'm not wearing a hat."

When we get back to her desk, she opens up a drawer, pulls out a hat that looks like a birthday cake with little foam candles on top of it, and sticks the hat on my head.

The hat is too small and squishes my forehead all funny.

"Now, you are fully equipped to hold on to your hat," Miss Jamie says, laughing.

I feel around on top of my head and grab onto one of the candles, which makes Miss Jamie laugh even harder. "What were we doing, Lester? Seeing you with that ridiculous cake on your head, I can't seem to remember anything."

"An advanced search?"

"Ah, yes." She looks back at the computer. "One of the most powerful tools at a librarian's disposal to locate the perfect material for our patrons. Now Lester, it sounds as if you are looking for a book that's both about kickball *and* also about some of the science behind the kicking."

"That's exactly what I want!"

"So, all we have to do is type *kickball* here and *science* here and switch this here and check this box here and voila!" She flings her hand up in the air. "Wait. That can't be right." She types and clicks, then looks up at me. "Nothing. Lester, I've failed you."

265

"It's okay, Miss Jamie." I hand her back the hat.

"It was so good to see you," she says. "Don't wait so long to come back again, okay?"

"All right, Miss Jamie." I walk out of the children's section to go find Mom. At least I found a book about the rules. That's something I couldn't figure out on my own.

"Lester!! Lester, wait!!" Miss Jamie runs toward me with a little paper in one hand and the birthday cake hat in the other. And she's yelling. Right in the middle of the library. "*Sports*, Lester. Kickball, kicking, kick—they were all too specific."

Everyone's looking at her, but she just keeps on yelling and running.

"I needed to generalize and search for 'sports' instead. I found one book, Lester. And blessings be, it's checked in." She shoves the hat back on my head, grabs my hand, and pulls me along after her. "We're journeying into the adult section, just like last spring when you were researching supernovas." We run past the adult reference desk, where Mom is standing. "Don't bother following us, Lucy," Miss Jamie says. "You couldn't keep up."

We turn down the second-to-last aisle of books and stop somewhere in the middle. She runs her finger along the numbers on the spines of the books and then stops. "That's funny. It should be right here. Oh, fiddlesticks. I can't let your hopes be shattered again because of misshelved materials."

She bends down so her eyes are level with the shelf, then

reaches over the books. "It's . . . here." She pulls something out. It's small and black and thick. She blows on it, and a bunch of dust comes flying off the cover.

Then Miss Jamie kneels down on one knee in front of me. "Lester, I present to you . . . *The Science of Sport.*"

I flip through the pages. There are science equations and math problems and drawings and diagrams of people running and throwing and hitting and kicking!

"This book is exactly what I need, Miss Jamie!"

"Oh, Lester, those words are music to a librarian's ears." She stands back up. "Now, I've done all I can. The rest is up to you."

Practice

WHEN I GET OUT TO THE KICKBALL FIELD ON MONDAY, ALL THE kids are standing in a big circle. It didn't say anything about circles in *Kickball: The Rules*, but if everyone's doing it, then it must be something I should do too.

I stand in an open spot next to Michael Z. "Why are we in a circle?"

"We count off to figure out who's fielding and who's kicking. Then that's what you are for the day. Ricky thinks switching wastes too much time."

"When you say switching, do you mean when the fielding team gets three outs and runs into their dugout and gets ready to kick while the team who just kicked runs out into the field and gets ready to be fielders?"

He looks at me funny. "What? Did you, like, go home and read a book about kickball over the weekend or something?"

"Two books, actually. But I didn't read most of the second one. It was really complicated and a lot of it wasn't even about kicking."

"Well, you can't read out here." He points to my lab notebook. "You have to focus on the game."

"This isn't a book for reading. It's my lab notebook for my kickball experiment." I open it and show him the diagram of the field. "I'm going to mark where each kick lands and write down other data about the kick in this chart."

"That's just like stats, Lester. My sister does that for her softball team."

Ricky runs into the circle carrying the kickball. "Let's count off," he says, and starts walking around pointing at kids. Everyone says either *one* or *two* depending on what the kid right before them said. He's walking fast and kids are counting fast. He's almost around to me and all of a sudden the only thing I can think of is that I'm all the way out here and Mrs. Raines is all the way over there and none of this feels like a good idea anymore.

Ricky points at Michael Z, and he says *one*.

Then Ricky points at me. It's too late to run away so I just say *two*.

He steps past me and points to Sydney.

That's it? He didn't call me Mussel-bum or say anything

mean. He just acted like I was any other kid.

"*Ones* are fielders. *Twos* are kickers," Ricky says after he finishes counting. "Let's go!"

Kids start running all around the field.

"Lester." Michael Z motions me over to him. "Just do whatever Ricky says and you'll be fine." Michael Z runs to stand by first base. Sydney stands between second and third. Ricky's on the pitcher's mound.

Since I'm a kicker, I run to the dugout and wait there for my turn to kick, just like it said I should in the book.

"Tori, you're up," Ricky yells.

She stands behind home plate and waits for the ball to get to her instead of running to meet it. Her kick rolls across the ground between Ricky and Michael Z. I mark the spot on my map where Ricky scoops up the ball. Then, on the chart next to her name, I write that she didn't run.

Connor's next. Instead of standing and waiting for the ball like Tori, Connor runs. His kick flies way out into the outfield again today. I mark the spot on the diagram and record the other data on my chart.

People keep kicking. I keep recording the data.

Three more kids to go until it's my turn.

Two more kids.

One more.

Just do whatever Ricky says and you'll be fine. I'll be fine. Everything will be fine.

270

"Come on, Mussel-bum," Ricky yells. "Let's get this over with."

I set my lab notebook on the bench and walk up to home plate. I don't stand too close, since I'm going to try one of those running kicks like Connor did.

Ricky rolls the ball. I start running. When I get to home plate, I swing my leg, but I'm too early. The ball rolls right under me.

"I get another chance," I tell Ricky. "That was only one strike which means I have two more chances because you're not out unless you get three strikes."

Ricky turns to Michael Z. "I told you."

"Just throw it to him again," Michael Z says. "He does get two more tries."

Ricky rolls his eyes around in his head and turns back to me. "Two more chances, Mussel-bum. You miss these and you're gone."

I got to home plate too early last time, which means I started running too early. This time I wait until the ball is rolling toward me to start running, and it works. The ball and I get to home plate at the exact same time. I swing my leg forward and my toes smash into the ball. It flies up into the air, straight over Ricky's head, and lands out in the grass.

I did it. I kicked the ball!

"Run!" someone yells from the dugout.

Right. Kick, then run. To first base. When I get there,

Michael Z is standing with his foot on the base waiting for someone to throw him the kickball, but the ball isn't there yet. I'm safe!

He high-fives me even though he's a fielder and I'm a kicker. "I knew you would be good, Lester."

"I did everything he said, but he still called me Mussel-bum and was mean when I missed the first kick."

"So?"

"You said when I found my thing, he'd start being nice to me."

"This is only the first day, Lester. You haven't proven anything yet. Just wait until he sees how good you get with a little practice."

That's true. And besides, right now every kick is just part of my experiment. Once I figure out how to kick the ball really far and help our class win the trophy, he'll stop calling me Mussel-bum and start being nice to me, just like he did with Michael Z when he found out how fast Michael Z could run.

Kicking Data

AFTER KICKING THE BALL A BUNCH OF DIFFERENT WAYS WITH Mom and analyzing the kicking data for over a week of recesses, I figure one thing out. The kids who run to kick the ball kick it farther than kids who don't. That means that Connor always kicks it farther than Tori, because he always runs and she doesn't. So I know that if I want to kick the ball as far as I possibly can, I need to run to kick it.

The problem is, not all of Connor's kicks go as far as his others. Some of them land in the front part of the outfield and others land farther back, closer to the fence. The same thing happens with my kicks even though I run and kick the ball just as hard each time. And scientifically, if I'm kicking them the same way each time, they should land in about the same place, just like my airplanes did.

"It just doesn't make sense, Mom!"

"Let's talk through it," Mom says. She's at the sink washing the dinner dishes, and I'm sitting here at the table trying not to tear the pages of this dumb experiment out of my lab notebook and rip them to shreds.

"It won't help, Mom. I've already tried thinking about it a bunch of different ways."

This has never happened before. Usually, I figure out my science experiments right away. I've been working on this for a week and a half, I still don't have a conclusion, and the kickball game is in two days.

Mom dries off her hands and comes over to me. "Just tell me what you know."

"I know that in my airplane experiment, when Abby threw the planes, all three planes of each type landed in about the same place, except for the medium-wing one that went behind the slide. But that was because of the wind."

"What else do you know?"

"I know that even though I run and kick as hard as I can and I do it in the exact same way each time, my kicks always land in different places."

"So, what does that mean?"

"That something else is happening!"

In my airplane experiment, the only variable was wing shape. That's why I had to wait for a windless day. But I don't think it's the wind that's making my kicks land in different places. I can make two kicks, one right after the other, and they still go different distances. I have to figure out what's happening.

I run in my room and grab *The Science of Sport* off my nightstand. I already read the whole kicking section when I first got the book over a week ago, but I haven't looked at it since. Maybe there's something in there I missed.

On the third page, I find my answer.

"Mom! Come quick!"

She runs into my room.

"There's another variable! It's not just about how hard I kick the ball, it's about how high the ball goes. Look." The diagram at the bottom of the page shows the path of three different kicks. The kicks that go really high and the kicks that go low don't go as far as the medium kicks.

"The path of the ball when it flies through the air, that's called an arc." Mom moves her hand in a curve like the shape of an upside-down bowl.

"So, if I want to kick the ball as far as I possibly can, I have to kick it in the middle in a perfect medium arc. That's my new hypothesis."

I run to the kitchen and put on my shoes. "Come on, Mom. We have to try it out."

After a few kicks, I figure out that I can make the ball fly in different arcs by kicking different spots on the ball. If my foot is more under the ball, my kick goes really high. If my foot kicks the ball more on its side, the ball flies in a low arc or rolls across the ground. But if I kick the ball just a little bit under it but kind of at the side, then it flies in the perfect medium arc, exactly like I need it to.

By the time it's dark and we have to go in, I'm pretty good at kicking the ball in the exact right spot. Most of my kicks land near the edge of the cornfield, which is really, really far away from where I'm kicking it. The medium-arc rule works.

I wonder if anyone else knows about it. Ricky probably does since he's such a good kicker. He's so good he doesn't even need to practice. That's why he's the full-time pitcher at recess.

Tomorrow I'll show him and everyone else. I'll run and kick the ball in a medium arc, and it will go farther than it's ever gone before. When Ricky sees how far it goes, I bet he'll stop calling me Mussel-bum right away.

The Medium-Arc Rule

WE NUMBER OFF AND I'M A KICKER AGAIN TODAY SO I SIT ON the bench, and I watch. Each time someone kicks, I check it against my conclusion. If the kicks are too high or too low, they don't go as far as the kicks that fly in a perfect medium arc. It's like every kick is proving my conclusion.

Connor walks up to the plate and waits. When Ricky throws the ball, Connor runs to meet it just like he's supposed to, but when he kicks the ball, the toe of his shoe is way too low and it catches on the edge of home plate. The ball makes a tiny little arc and lands on the ground right in front of Ricky. Connor falls on his hands and knees in front of home plate.

"What an easy out," Ricky says, and throws the ball to Michael Z. Some of the other kids are laughing, but Connor's still on the ground. He finally gets up and runs off the field.

I'm up. This is it. This is my chance to finally show everyone what I learned in my experiment. I walk up to home plate then back up a few steps and wait. Ricky throws the ball. When it's halfway to the plate, I run. My foot remembers exactly what it did last night and kicks the ball in the exact right spot, which means that it leaves my foot and flies in a perfect medium arc.

But that's not the only thing that leaves my foot. My shoe flies right past Ricky and lands at the edge of the outfield. But the ball keeps going, way way into the outfield. It finally lands, bounces a few times, and rolls into the fence.

I kicked it to the fence.

"Run!" Michael Z yells.

"But my shoe—"

"RUN!" he screams.

So, with only one shoe on, I take off toward first. When I get there, the ball is still way out in the field. I keep going.

To second.

To third.

Les-ter. Les-ter. Les-ter.

They're cheering my name. And it's not just the kids waiting to kick. It's the kids on the field too.

When I round third, someone in the outfield is throwing the ball to Ricky, but he doesn't have it yet, which means I don't have to stop. So, I keep running, straight over home plate.

A home run! And it's all because of my kickball experiment.

"Aw, yeah! Everyone remembers who discovered him, right?" Michael Z yells across the field. "Just two weeks of practice and he already kicks it to the fence."

Sydney grabs my shoe from the outfield and throws it to Ricky. He holds it by the toe and shakes it around. The sole is so broken the whole shoe wiggles back and forth. "You were kicking in this trash?" he says, and throws it at me.

"You're just jealous," Connor yells from the dugout.

"Jealous?" Ricky laughs. "Have you seen my shoes?" He holds up his foot. He's still wearing those bright red shoes that come up to his ankles, the ones I first saw way back in the library when Ricky was doing his math and I was doing my school research.

"No," Connor says. "Jealous that you're not the best kicker anymore. Even with those broken shoes he kicked it all the way to the fence."

Ricky looks at me. "It was just one kick."

Connor shrugs. "When's the last time you kicked it to the fence?"

"I can't kick when I'm pitching."

"I could pitch," Connor says. "I bet the whole class would love to see you kick."

The kids all cheer again.

"I guess I could take a second to kick, you know, to show everyone how it's *really* done," Ricky says.

I grab my shoe off the ground and run back to the dugout to watch.

Ricky stands behind home plate exactly where I did. He runs to meet the ball, and when he kicks, it goes almost straight up into the air. The arc is really high, which means his foot was too far under the ball. It lands right in Connor's arms on the pitcher's mound.

"Out!" Connor yells.

"That was just a warm-up," Ricky yells back. "Throw it again."

Connor throws and Ricky kicks and this time it goes into the outfield, but not very far because the arc is still too high. Maybe . . . no. Ricky knows everything there is to know about kickball. Surely, he has to know the medium-arc rule.

"I thought you were going to kick it to the fence," Connor yells.

"I am. I was just showing you what not to do. Throw it again."

Connor throws the ball again and Ricky kicks again and it goes really far into the outfield. But not as far as mine.

"You're kicking it too high," I say.

"What?" he yells back.

"You have to kick the ball in a medium arc if you want it to go really far like mine did." I show him with my hand like Mom showed me last night.

Ricky stares at me. Connor stares at me. Everyone's staring at me. It's like no one understands what I'm saying.

"I did an experiment about it." I grab my lab notebook from the bench and show Ricky the diagram I drew last night of a little foot kicking a ball in the exact right spot. "Your foot is too far under the ball. That's why the ball goes really high in the air but not all the way to the fence."

"He's giving you advice, Ricky!" Connor says, laughing.

"Are you seriously telling me how to kick, Mussel-bum?" Ricky yells.

"Your foot was in the wrong place. That's why my kick went to the fence and—"

"Get off my field." He grabs my lab notebook and throws it as hard as he can over the fence.

My experiments!

I run to see if it's okay. A bunch of the pages are bent and it's got grass stains on it, but at least the pages aren't ripped.

"You too, Mini-Mike," Ricky yells from the field.

"But I didn't tell him to say that!"

"We all remember who discovered him. You! Which means it's your fault he's out here."

Michael Z runs off the field straight over to me. "Are you insane?"

"I was just trying to help."

"By telling Ricky, the best kicker in the class, how to kick?"

"But he can't be the best kicker if he's doing it wrong! Look!" I open my lab notebook to show him the diagram, but he slams it closed.

"You just don't get it, do you?"

"Get what?"

"Ricky's always the best at sports. He's even better than Connor. Don't tell Connor I said that. But he is."

"I was just trying to help him be even better!"

Michael Z kicks the grass with his foot. "He called me Mini-Mike, Lester. He hasn't called me that in over a year."

Ricky yells at someone on the field. He's not just mad at us. He's mad at everyone.

Michael Z turns away from me and walks toward the bleachers.

"Wait!" I run after him.

"Don't follow me, Lester." He holds his hand up like a policeman telling someone to stop. "I'm done."

"With what?"

"You."

He climbs the bleachers and sits in the last row with his back to me.

I sit down on the ground in the same spot my medium-wing airplanes landed when Abby threw them from the top of the curly slide. Science experiments may take a long time to do and they can be really hard sometimes, but I can always, always, always figure them out.

People aren't like science experiments at all.

One second they're cheering for you and the next second they're saying they're done with you.

One minute they're watching you make a perfect kick, a kick that could help your team win the big game tomorrow, and the next minute they're throwing you off the kickball field.

One day they're acting like they're your best friend and the next day when someone new comes along they stop talking to you and stop swinging with you and don't even eat lunch with you anymore.

"Lester?" Mrs. Raines says. She isn't by her tree anymore. "What's wrong?"

I try to think of words to explain it but my brain is spinning with all these thoughts and I feel like I can't breathe.

"Why don't you go take a break in Mr. Jacobsen's room?"

That's exactly what I need. To get away from everything out here. I jump up off the ground and run toward the door, but I have to stop and run back when my shoe falls off again.

Stupid broken shoe.

I don't even try putting it back on my foot. I just carry it with me until I'm safe in Beanbag Beach.

Break

MR. JACOBSEN WALKS AROUND THE CORNER OF THE BOOKCASE. "That shoe's seen better days."

"It won't even stay on my foot anymore."

"I can imagine." He laughs. Then he asks me what's going on.

"You never come over here and ask me that. You always let me come to you when I'm ready to talk."

He kneels down beside me. "I'm going to be busy in a little bit. So, if you want to talk, we need to do it now."

I tell him about my experiment and how I learned to kick really far and about how I tried to help Ricky with his kick and how he got mad.

"Can you think of a reason why giving him advice would make him mad?"

"No."

"Lester, I want you to think about something." Mr. Jacobsen looks behind him, then back to me. "What if Ricky won the science fair instead of you?"

Thinking about that makes me laugh. "That would never happen. I'm the best at science."

"Lester, that's how Ricky feels about kickball."

I stop laughing because it doesn't feel funny anymore.

Mr. Jacobsen stands up.

"Ricky kicked me off the field. Does that mean I can't play tomorrow?"

"No, Lester. You get to play."

"Good, because if I didn't, that would be like doing a whole science fair project and not actually getting to be in the science fair."

"I think you might need some different shoes, though," Mr. Jacobsen says, and looks at the clock. "All right, Lester. Since you seem to be feeling better now, why don't you head on back to class?"

"Why do you want me to leave so fast?"

"I'm getting ready to work with someone else."

"But there're always lots of kids in here at the same time. It never mattered before."

The sound of metal hitting metal echoes through the room, like a chair hitting the leg of a table. Someone else is here.

Mr. Jacobsen walks around the corner of Beanbag Beach toward the front of the room. "How're you doing today, buddy?"

Whoever's in the chair doesn't say anything.

"I thought we'd take a break from multiplication for a couple of days and review subtraction."

"Why?"

I recognize the voice but peek around the corner just to be sure. I knew it. Ricky's here.

"It's always good to review, and I found this fun Halloween worksheet," Mr. Jacobsen says. "Let's start with this one. Show me what you'd do first."

Ricky doesn't have time to show Mr. Jacobsen anything because the phone rings and Mr. Jacobsen answers it. "Yes, he's still down here . . . I'm not sure how long." Mr. Jacobsen hangs up the phone.

"Who's here?" Ricky asks.

I jump back into my beanbag and try not to breathe.

Ricky walks around the corner of the bookcase, then turns back around and disappears. I wait for him to come back around the corner and start yelling at me, but he doesn't.

When I peek around the corner again, he's sitting down with his head on the table.

"Ricky," Mr. Jacobsen says, "please sit up."

"He's going to tell people," Ricky says.

"Tell people what?" Mr. Jacobsen asks.

"That I'm doing baby math."

"Don't call it that, Ricky. You know we all have our struggles. I didn't start reading—"

"Until fifth grade!" Ricky yells. "Yeah, Mr. Jacobsen. You've told me that dumb old story a million times. But guess what? Knowing that you were stupid too doesn't help!"

Mr. Jacobsen walks around the bookcase. "Lester, I think it'd be best if you go back to your room now."

This time, I don't argue. Ricky is madder than I've ever seen him before. He's so mad he's yelling at a teacher, which is something you're never allowed to do. Ever.

I walk out of the room as fast as I can. As soon as I'm out in the hallway, I realize my shoe is still in there. But it doesn't matter because it's broken, and Mom's going to have to get me a new pair anyway. The only other shoes I have are my brown dress-up ones, and I can't play in the kickball game in those.

Shoes

WHEN I COME OUT TO THE CAR WITH ONE SHOE, MOM MAKES me go back in for the other one. She says I can't go to the shoe store and walk around in a public place without both of my shoes on. So I go back in and get it because we have to go to the shoe store tonight.

It takes almost an hour to get to the mall and find a parking spot and walk all the way to the shoe store, which is really far away from the mall doors. And it takes even longer because I keep walking out of my shoe. But when we get there, all the walking and losing my shoe was worth it.

There's a poster in the window, twice as tall as I am that says: *Run faster. Jump higher. Kick harder. Be a SUPERSTAR.* Blue stars are shooting out of the words.

Under the poster is a pair of shoes unlike any other shoes I've ever seen before. They're shiny like the poster itself and look like they would come up to my ankles! On each side of the shoe is a blue star, just like the ones on the poster.

But the shininess and the star aren't even the most amazing part. The bottoms of the shoes don't have designs or patterns on them. The sole of the left shoe says the word *SUPER* and the right sole says the word *STAR*. Behind the glass is a bunch of sand showing how it would look if you walked across it wearing those shoes. Every step with the left foot writes *super* and every step with the right foot writes *star—super star, super star, super star.*

"Mom!"

She's shaking her head.

"I can't get them?"

"What?"

"Why are you shaking your head, Mom?"

"I just can't believe these shoes exist."

"Yesterday they didn't." A man wearing a black-and-white-striped shirt walks around the corner. "Today is the very first day they're available."

"It says *kick harder* on the sign. Do they really make you kick harder?"

"The triple-reinforced toe box provides your foot with the perfect kicking surface. If that won't help with your kicking, I don't know what will."

"Did you hear that, Mom? They have a triple-reinforced toe box. I'll probably kick even better tomorrow."

"Uh-huh," she says.

"Would you like to try on a new pair of Superstars?" he asks me.

"Yes! Yes! Yes!"

Mom tells the man my size, and he goes into the back of the store. Mom and I sit on a red bench and wait for him.

He comes out a few seconds later with a blue box. "These are new for the holiday season," the man says.

"I didn't know they sold shoes for Halloween," Mom says.

"No, ma'am. The Christmas season." He takes the lid off the box, but I can't see my shoes yet because they are covered in tissue paper.

"But it's only October," Mom says.

"People want to start early these days. Be done by Thanksgiving. You know?"

I hold my foot up in his face.

"A little excited, aren't we?" the man says.

"Yes, but it doesn't seem like you are," I say to him.

"Patience, grasshopper. Patience."

He just called me grasshopper, but I don't even care why because he pulls one of the shoes out of the box and holds it up. It's just as shiny as the example shoe in the window. It's tall and puffy like a boot but it looks like a sneaker. He turns it over and carved into the rubber is the word *SUPER*. He puts my left foot on a little angled stool, then slides it into the shoe, and I'm wearing it! I'm wearing the *SUPER*. I jump up and start walking around.

"Don't you want the other one?"

Oh yeah. The other shoe. I sit back down and put my other foot out. He holds the shoe up. *STAR* is carved into the bottom of it.

Then he ties the laces for me, even though I know how to tie them myself, and asks me to stand up. He pushes down on my toe and then squeezes around the sides of my foot. "They seem to fit really well with a little room for growing. Walk around the store and see how they feel."

I step up on a bench. With just a little jump, I can probably make it to the sand in the window. The man runs over and holds his arm out in front of me. "You can't go in the sand."

"But we don't have any sand at home, and I want to test them out."

"Don't worry. They work in dirt, too."

"How do they feel on your feet?" Mom asks.

"They're the most wonderful, perfect, amazing shoes ever invented!"

She puts her arms on my shoulders, so I have to face her. "But do they *feel* good?"

"Yes, Mom. Yes. Yes. Yes. I could walk for ten miles and my

feet would feel like they just got out of bed in the morning."

Mom looks at the man. "Do I dare ask how much they are?"

"Only $99.99 plus tax. They're on sale. This week only. Next week they'd cost you $119.99."

"One hundred twenty dollars for a pair of shoes for a ten-year-old?"

"These aren't just any shoes, ma'am. They're Superstars."

"Yes, I'm aware of the name. Sir, if you would please give us a minute." Mom pulls me over to the bench and sits me down next to her.

"Please, Mom! Please, please, please! These are the perfect shoes for me and for kickball and for everything."

Mom looks down at my feet and then back to my face. "Here's the deal, Lester. I will buy you these shoes now, but we will be partaking in our first and last bit of holiday-season shopping described by this gentleman earlier and you will be receiving $99.99 plus tax less of Christmas presents this year, which means that you might just be getting some fruit for Christmas."

"Deal!" I reach out to shake her hand but she pulls it away too quickly.

"And you're not allowed to grow out of them. Ever!"

"Mom, I can't stop growing."

She puts her arms around me and starts squeezing. "What if I hold you like this forever?"

"Mom!"

"Okay, Lester. But these really do count as a Christmas present. Is that a deal?"

I hold my hand out to her again. As soon as we shake, the man is standing right next to us again.

"Would you like me to box them up?"

"Are you kidding me?" Mom says. "I'll be lucky to get them off when he goes to bed tonight."

"Don't worry, Mom. I don't sleep in shoes except on meteor shower nights."

He puts my old shoes in the box, and we all walk to the counter. After we pay, Mom and I walk out of the store, right past the shoe poster.

I'm wearing those shoes. Right now. They're on my feet.

Get ready, dirt. Here I come!

Footprints

BY THE TIME WE GET HOME, IT'S DARK, BUT I DON'T CARE. I jump out of the car and run straight to the flower garden.

Left foot. *Super.*

Right foot. *Star.*

Left foot. *Super.*

Right foot. *Star.*

I look behind me, but it's too dark to tell if it's working. "Mom! I can't see anything out here!"

A minute later, Mom comes outside and shines a flashlight on the ground behind me. The words are written in the dirt. *Super. Star. Super. Star.*

"Mom, they work!"

With the flashlight, I kneel down and inspect the letters

more closely. Since the words are carved into the shoes, when I take a step, the dirt gets pushed up into the bottom of the soles to form the letters. So, the words actually look like they're coming up out of the ground.

I run over to Mom and give her a hug. "Thank you so much."

Mom hugs me back. "Lester, I was thinking. Do you want to sit out here and watch the sky with me for a bit?"

Except for the Perseid meteor shower every August, we never sit outside and watch the stars, especially when it's cold like it is tonight.

I run inside the house and grab the outside blanket from the hall closet, and Mom and I go out to the middle of the yard where we always watch the superstars.

"Do you remember when you started calling them super-stars, Lester?"

"Sort of." Actually, I remember the exact moment, but if I say that, she won't tell me the story.

"Well, you had just turned four."

I stare up into the starry blackness.

"That was the year your dad gave you that Superman suit. And everything you did was Superman. You two watched the cartoons and played together and pretended to save your other toys. He used to fly you all over that little yard we had down there." Mom laughs. "And when he wasn't flying you around, you were flying your little Superman around. And that year when we went to watch the meteor shower . . ."

"I wore my Superman suit. And we had those chairs that laid back so we didn't have to lay on the ground."

"I don't know what happened to those," Mom says. "They'd be way more comfortable than lying on this blanket like we do now."

"Mom. Back to the story!"

"Well, back then, you always watched the superstars on your dad's lap. He'd pull you up so your cheeks were touching and you'd be looking right where he was looking, right at the very same piece of sky."

"But I didn't sit with him for long, did I?"

"As soon as that first meteor shot across the sky, Lester, you jumped up and started running circles around us yelling, 'It's a bird. It's a plane. It's a superstar!' And we've called them superstars ever since."

"Mom!"

"Yeah?"

"You're looking at me."

"I know."

"But you can't look at me. You have to keep your eyes on the sky. If you don't and there's a superstar, you'll miss it."

"I doubt we'll see one tonight. Superstars are pretty rare when there's not a meteor shower."

"Have you ever seen one?"

"Just once. It was the night your dad and I graduated from

college. We were taking one last walk across campus, and right when we were passing the clock tower we both stopped and looked up and there it was."

"Was it big and really bright?"

"No. It was a little dim, and it didn't stay in the sky for long. But we both saw it."

"I wish there would be one right now."

Mom grabs ahold of my hand, even though we didn't see one. "Do you remember what your dad always said, Lester? How the moment has to be just right?"

Mom and I are out here looking at the sky for the first time in months. She told me the superstar story. I just got my new Superstar shoes with the triple-reinforced toe box that are going to help me make the best kick of my whole entire life tomorrow.

I know that none of that has anything to do with bits of space dust flying into the earth's atmosphere, but this moment sure does feel like a just-right moment.

We wait.

And we wait.

And we wait.

Finally, when we're both shivering, Mom says we have to go inside. I watch the sky all the way to the door, but there aren't any.

Tonight, the only Superstars are the ones on my feet.

Superstars

I'M NOT EVEN IN MY SEAT FOR FIVE SECONDS BEFORE MICHAEL Z grabs my foot and lifts it up in the air. "You got Superstars?" He rubs his finger over the bottom of my shoe.

"You know about them?"

"No way!" Connor leans down and grabs my other foot. I have to hold on to my desk so I don't fall off my chair. "These just came out yesterday."

"That's when I got them."

More and more kids crowd around my desk until it seems like the whole class is here. Kids are grabbing my feet and running their fingers over the words carved in the bottoms.

"Ricky, come here," Connor yells across the room.

When Ricky doesn't come, Connor grabs my arm and

pulls me out of my chair through the crowd of kids over to Ricky's desk. When we get there, he lifts my foot up and holds it right in front of Ricky's face. "Feel the bottom. It's just like they showed on TV."

Ricky knocks my foot out of Connor's hand. "I don't care about his stupid shoes."

My foot bangs against the edge of Ricky's desk, which probably would hurt if the whole inside of my shoe didn't feel like it was covered in pillows.

"Whatever," Connor says, and walks away.

I leave too. The last place I want to be is over here next to Ricky, especially when Mrs. Raines isn't in the room.

"Nice shoes," Abby says when I walk by her desk. "They'd be perfect for your superhero chic design." Abby's holding a picture of a baby. Even though he's dressed up like a pumpkin, I recognize him right away. "That's Charlie."

"You remember his name?"

"Of course I do."

She holds the picture out to me. "My mom and I made this costume for him."

His body is covered in a puffy orange ball, and he's wearing a little green hat with a leaf on it. "He looks so much bigger. And not just because he's dressed like a pumpkin."

"I know, Lester. He's growing so fast. Sometimes he looks bigger when I get home from school than he did in the morning. And he doesn't cry so much either."

Mona slides onto her chair and grabs the picture out of my hand. "Who's the pumpkin?"

"It's Charlie," Abby says.

"Okay. And who's Charlie?" Mona asks.

How can Mona not know about Charlie?

"He's my baby brother, Mona. I told you about him lots of times."

Mona shrugs. "Guess where I went last night!"

Abby turns away from Mona and stares down at the picture.

"Come on, Abby. Guess."

But Abby doesn't guess. She doesn't say anything.

Mona opens a folder from her backpack and pulls out a piece of blue cardboard with a picture of rainbow-colored sparkly wings on it. "I finally got my mom to take me to the Halloween store. We bought these for my costume." She holds the picture in front of Abby. "Look how perfect they are."

Abby turns around. "What about the wings *I* made you?"

"These new ones are way better. Just wait until you see them on me tonight." Mona looks up at me and makes the noise like she's got something stuck in her throat, which means she's about to tell me to leave. But this time I go before she can say anything. I've got a lot more important things to do than listen to her talk about some dumb wings anyway.

When I get back to my seat, Connor lifts up my foot again. "Do they really make prints in the dirt?"

"They did in my garden last night."

"I'm totally getting a pair this weekend," Connor says, and holds his hand up like he's about to give me a high five. I hold my hand up too, just in case, and that's exactly what he does.

"Me, too. I'm getting them, too," Michael Z says, and high-fives me.

Connor and Michael Z both just gave me high fives and all I did was get these shoes. Wait until they see me kick in them.

The Kickball Game

WHEN OUR CLASS GETS OUTSIDE, WE ALL STAND ALONG THE fence inside the dugout while Ricky tells us the kicking lineup.

"When I call your name," Ricky yells, "go sit on the bench in that order."

He's first. Then Connor. Then Sydney. They go sit down.

Then Michael Z. Then Mona. I wait and wait and wait. Ricky calls more and more kids, but none of them are me.

Finally, he calls Michael H. Then Tori. And Abby.

They all go sit down. Then Ricky goes and sits down.

"What about me?" I yell at him.

"Oh. I must have forgot about you." He laughs. "You're last."

"Welcome to the Quarry Kickball Classic," Mr. Marmel yells into his megaphone.

The kids in the bleachers cheer.

"And just like every year, the winning team will return to their classroom with the coveted Quarry Kickball Cup."

Mr. Jacobsen stands up in the first row of bleachers and holds the trophy up for everyone to see. It's gold like my science fair trophy but twice as tall, and it's actually shaped like a cup.

"Now, who's ready to play some kickball?" Mr. Marmel says.

Both classes cheer.

"Mrs. Raines's class, let's get some players out here on this empty field! And Mrs. Turner's class, yoooooooou're up!"

Ricky and a bunch of the other kids run out to the field. Mrs. Raines walks over to me. "Lester? Are you one of the fielders?"

"No."

"Then why don't you go sit down and watch?"

"Because I'm last. I might not ever get a turn to kick all the way down there."

"In this game, everyone gets to kick, Lester. That's one of the rules." She puts her arm around my shoulder. "And besides, if you're at the end, you might just have a chance to make the game-winning kick."

I step backward. *Super star* is written in the dirt. "Look at the ground."

She looks down. "I'd say that's a pretty good sign, Lester."

I take two steps. *Super star.* And another two steps. *Super star.* I write it all the way over to Abby. *Super star. Super star. Super star. Super star.*

"Those shoes are kind of the best," Abby says when I sit down.

"They're not just kind of the best. They are the best. They even have a triple-reinforced toe box and everything." I hold my foot up. "It's the perfect kicking surface."

As we sit there and watch the game, I tell Abby more about my shoes and about my kicking experiment and explain how she should kick the ball when it's her turn to kick, and Abby tells me more about Charlie and her Halloween costume and how her mom helped her sew it. By the time the fielders get three outs and it's our turn to kick, it kind of feels like it did back when we used to go on the swings together every day.

"All right," Ricky says. "Watch and learn." He runs out to home plate, and on his way there, he waves at all the kids in the bleachers.

Olivia, who sits in Michael Z's seat during math, is the pitcher for the other team. "Easy out!" she yells to her team-mates.

"Yeah right," Ricky says. "You better tell them to back up."

But Olivia doesn't tell her team anything. Instead, she throws the ball fast and hard toward Ricky. He runs to meet the ball and kicks it straight into right field in a perfect medium arc, not too high and not too low. It flies way past the right fielder's head, and doesn't stop until it hits the fence. By the time the ball is almost back to Olivia, Ricky is a few steps away from third base and our class is screaming so loud I have to put my fingers in my ears.

Right as Ricky runs past third, Olivia catches the ball, then turns and throws it at him. He jumps back onto third right before the ball hits him.

"Safe," Mr. Marmel yells, and my class cheers again.

After a few more kickers, there isn't as much screaming because most people only make it to first or second. And then the other class gets three outs and it's their team that's screaming, but that doesn't bother me at all since they're way over on the other side of the field.

Abby and I sit there and watch the game.

"Hey, Lester," Abby says after a while.

"What?"

"Did you ever make an astronaut costume to go with your dad's helmet?"

"No."

"Do you want to? If you had a costume, then you could go trick-or-treating."

"Halloween's tonight, Abby."

"So?" She pulls a drawing of me out of her back pocket. It's a picture of me wearing a helmet and a space suit and my Superstar shoes. I didn't even think of that before. My new shoes are white and puffy, just like space boots.

"I don't have a suit, Abby."

"Do you have snow pants and a coat?"

"They're black. Space suits are supposed to be white."

"Lester, just have your mom take you to the painting store after school and buy one of those white zip-up suits that painters wear. Put that over your coat and snow pants, and you've got a space suit."

That does sounds like it would work.

"The only thing I haven't figured out yet is gloves," Abby says.

"My mom has white snow gloves."

"Lester, that's perfect. Oh, this is just going to be so great. I can't wait to see what you look like."

"How are you going to see me?"

"When we go trick-or-treating!" she says, smiling.

"We're going together?"

"Well, yeah . . . I mean, if you want to."

No one's ever invited me to go trick-or-treating with them before. No one's ever invited me to do anything with them before.

"Plus, if you come over, you could see Charlie in his pumpkin costume. And I promise, he really doesn't cry as much now."

I want to say yes. I really do, but Abby's going trick-or-treating with Mona, which means I'd be going trick-or-treating with Mona, and I'd rather stay home than do that.

"Abby, I can't."

"Okay," she says, and looks away.

Abby doesn't say anything else and neither do I. We just sit there and watch the game. Every time our class scores some runs the other class scores more runs and catches up to us. If I wanted to make a hypothesis about who's going to win that trophy, I wouldn't be able to. The scores are always so close together.

"Are you mad at me?" Abby asks after our class runs out to the field for the fourth time. "Is that why you don't want to come tonight?"

"No. I do want to come. I just don't want to go trick-or-treating with Mona."

"Me neither." Abby laughs and turns toward me. "Lester, she's not coming."

"But this morning, she said—"

"Yeah. And she also said that some dumb store-bought wings were better than the ones I made her. So, will you come?"

The only problem left is Mom. "Remember what my mom said, Abby?"

"Lester, you're not *being* an astronaut. You're just dressing up like one. And besides, she gave you your dad's space helmet."

That's true. It's sitting on my dresser right now. And she did tell me the story about superstars last night.

"She'll say yes, Lester. I know she will. I'll have my mom call her and work out everything." She kicks her foot against

307

the side of my shoe and points out to the field.

Our class is running in.

"Lester, I think it's time."

"What an exciting game so far!" Mr. Marmel says into his megaphone. "Mrs. Turner's class is in the lead with seventeen. Mrs. Raines's class is close behind with fifteen. And we're in the final inning, kids. Since Mrs. Turner's class kicked first, Mrs. Raines's class gets one more chance. Will they score the three runs they need to win or will Mrs. Turner's class hold the lead? It's still anyone's game!!!"

Michael H was the last one to kick. That means there's Tori, then Abby, then me. We need three runs to win, and I'm third. It's just like Mrs. Raines said. I could make the game-winning kick.

Ricky runs down to our end of the bench and leans down in front of us. "Here's what you guys need to do. Just kick it nice and low and get onto base. Then the lineup will start over, and I'll kick you all in."

"You won't need to kick, Ricky. If Tori and Abby get on base, and I get a home run like I did yesterday, we'll have eighteen points already."

"No," Ricky says.

"Yes," I say. "They have seventeen, so when we get eighteen, we win."

"I know that, Mussel-BUM. I just . . ." He looks at Abby. "Ugh. Never mind." Ricky walks down to his end of the bench.

He doesn't sit down, though. He just stands by the fence at the front of the dugout, staring at me.

"That was weird," Abby says, "even for him."

"Mrs. Raines's class," Mr. Marmel yells from the field. "We need a kicker."

Tori runs up to home plate. She kicks a low one, straight toward third base, and makes it safe to first.

Then it's Abby's turn. She stands behind the plate and runs to kick the ball, just like I told her, but her foot must have hit it in the wrong place because her kick flies in a high arc in the air, straight toward Olivia. But Olivia doesn't catch it. It slips out of her hands, bounces off her foot, and rolls toward home plate.

Abby runs to first. Tori runs to second. They're both safe.

I press my shoes down into the dirt, then lift them up. There it is. *Super star.*

With each step toward home plate, I say the words that my feet are writing. "Super star. Super star." I go faster. "Superstar. Superstar." And faster. "Superstar, superstar." And even faster. "Superstar superstar superstar stuperstar stuperstar st—"

"*Stuper* star?" Ricky says when I walk by him. "More like *stupid* star."

I keep right on walking, out of the dugout and onto the field, and Ricky follows right behind me. "*Stupid* star. *Stupid* star. *Stupid* star," he says with each step I take.

"Stop saying that!" I turn around and yell at him.

Mr. Marmel runs over to us. "Ricky, are you trying to get

yourself kicked out of this game?"

"No." He looks down at the ground.

"Then get yourself back to the dugout." Mr. Marmel turns to me and smiles really big. "Lester, I believe it is *finally* your turn to kick."

Mr. Marmel walks back toward home plate. I start to follow, but stop when I hear my name.

Not *stupid* star. Not Mussel-bum. Not Mouse Boy or baby.

"Lester?" Ricky says again.

"Yeah?" I turn around.

"Let me do it."

"Do what?"

He reaches up and wipes across his eyes with the back of his hand.

Ricky's crying? But he shouldn't be sad. We didn't lose the game. In fact, we're about to win. And if he hadn't called me *stupid* star and followed me out here, we probably would have won by now.

He takes a step closer to me and talks in a voice so low that I can barely hear it. "Just get onto base. Let me kick you guys in." He looks right at me, and I look right back at him. "Please?" he says.

"Ricky!" Mr. Marmel says from behind home plate and points to the dugout. "Go!"

Ricky turns and runs back to the dugout.

By the time I get to home plate, my class isn't sitting on the bench anymore. They're standing at the front of the dugout, and they're all cheering for me.

Everyone except Ricky. He's in his spot on the end of the bench leaning his head against the fence and staring at the trophy that Mr. Jacobsen's holding.

What if Ricky won the science fair instead of you? Mr. Jacobsen said yesterday.

But that would never happen, I told Mr. Jacobsen. *I'm the best at science.*

That's how Ricky feels about kickball.

"Stop! Wait!" I yell, right as Olivia swings her arm back and throws the ball.

The ball flies out of her hand, bounces off to the side of me, and hits the fence.

"Oh, come on!" Olivia yells.

I run and grab the ball. If my foot hits here, the ball flies in a perfect medium arc. If my foot hits too far under, the ball goes really high. So, to kick it low, I need to kick more on the side of the ball.

"Lester, can I have the ball, please?" Mr. Marmel asks.

I hand it to him. "I just needed to figure something out real fast."

He throws it to Olivia, and right away, she swings her arm back and throws the ball to me. I kick a little higher up on the ball than I usually do, and as soon as it leaves my foot, I know I kicked in the exact right place. The ball flies low and bounces right between the two kids playing first and second base. It doesn't stop rolling until it gets to the right fielder.

Tori runs. Abby runs. I run. The right fielder grabs the ball and throws it in to Olivia, but by the time the ball gets to her, we're all on base. Safe.

They're not cheering for me anymore. Michael Z even has his arms crossed like he's mad at me. But that's because he doesn't understand. He never understood. Kickball isn't my thing.

It's Ricky's.

"And with the winning run on first," Mr. Marmel yells into his megaphone, "we're starting the lineup again. Ricky, you're up."

Ricky runs up to home plate. A few seconds later, we're all chanting his name. Even some of the kids in the bleachers are doing it.

Olivia turns around and yells to her team to back up. Everyone in the outfield takes a few steps backward.

Ricky stands behind home plate and leans over a little. As soon as Olivia pitches, he starts running and kicks the ball in a perfect medium arc way above Olivia's head and over the center fielder's head and it's going farther than any kick I've ever seen before. Even mine.

"Lester, go!" Ricky screams.

I was watching his kick and forgot to run. Again.

"Lester!!!"

I fling my legs out in front of me and pump my arms. The little pillows in my shoes spring me forward with each step. I touch second base, then run toward third.

I look back for a split second. Ricky's right behind me.

"Keep going!" he screams.

We touch third, then it's straight down the third base line to home plate.

I step on it.

Ricky steps on it.

And all of a sudden we're jumping up and down, me and Ricky and Abby and Tori, we're jumping and screaming, and then the rest of the class comes out of the dugout and we're all jumping and screaming together.

Finally, Mr. Marmel yells into his megaphone and says we have to stop so we can get our trophy. We line up across the center of the field in our kicking order, and Mr. Jacobsen brings the trophy onto the field. He hands the trophy to Ricky first. Then Ricky passes it to Connor, and Connor passes it to Michael Z, and everyone passes it down the line so we all get to hold it. Finally, it gets to me. Since there's no one else to pass it on to, I just hold it up over my head.

Mr. Marmel sets his megaphone on the ground and starts clapping. Then Mrs. Raines starts clapping and Mr. Jacobsen and everyone in the stands and everyone in my class.

Even Ricky.

Costume

ABBY WAS RIGHT ABOUT EVERYTHING. MOM SAYS I CAN BE AN astronaut for Halloween and go trick-or-treating. And putting the painter's suit over my snow stuff looks just like a space suit.

After I get everything on, Mom helps me with my shoes and my gloves and finally my helmet.

I go into the hallway so I can see myself in the long mirror on the bathroom door. I really do look just like an astronaut. Like Dad.

Mom walks up behind me. She puts her hands on my shoulders and leans her chin on top of my helmet so we look like an astronaut with an extra Mom head on top.

"You remind me so much of him," she says.

"That's just because I'm wearing his helmet."

She shakes her head. "No, Lester. It's you. The things you say. The way you are." Mom wipes her eyes.

"Mom, no. Please don't cry."

She runs down the hallway into her room and closes the door.

In a tiny little corner of my brain, I thought it might be different now. After we found the trunk and she gave me the picture and the helmet and told me the story last night.

But it's not different. And right now, she's in her room—

Her door opens.

"Mom, I'm sorry. We can put the helmet back if you want to."

"Lester, stop." She walks into the hallway holding a box. A black leather box.

I've only seen it twice before in my life. One time was the other night when we went through the trunk. The other time was in Washington, DC.

She opens it and takes out Dad's medal.

"Mom? What are you doing?"

"I have to take it out of the box before I pin it on you, don't I?"

"But you can't think about this. It makes you too sad because of all the bad memories."

She unhooks the little metal pin on the back of the ribbon and sticks it through the white fabric on the right side of my chest. Then she clicks the pin closed.

"I think it's time for a new memory now."

Trick-or-Treating

BY THE TIME WE PULL INTO ABBY'S DRIVEWAY, IT'S MOSTLY dark. Abby and her mom are sitting on the porch in big rocking chairs waiting for us.

I jump out of the car, pull my helmet out of the backseat, and put it on my head. When I turn around, Abby's there. Her dress is long and black and flowy. It looks just like the picture she drew.

"Lester, that helmet is amazing, and . . ." Abby reaches out toward Dad's medal, then stops. "Can I touch it?"

I look over at Mom. She didn't say whether or not people could touch it.

"Go ahead," Mom says.

Abby runs her finger down the purple ribbon and around

the edge of the gold circle. She's probably thinking the same thing I am—that she can't believe Dad's medal is actually pinned to my chest.

"Your dress is beautiful, Abby," Mom says. "It reminds me of a dress I used to have."

"She designed it herself," I tell Mom.

Abby twirls around. The bottom of the dress flows out in a circle around her.

We all walk up onto the porch where Abby's mom is sitting and rocking Charlie in his pumpkin suit.

"My husband's off with the other two, Lucy," Abby's mom says. "I'm going to stay here with this little one and hand out candy if you want to stay and help?"

"Only if you let me hold him," Mom says.

Abby's mom hands Charlie to Mom. "I haven't held a baby in so long." She sits down in the other rocking chair with Charlie. "You know, Lester, you used to be this little once."

"We're going now." Abby grabs my hand and pulls me down the steps toward the sidewalk. As soon as we get to a house with the porch light on, we ring the doorbell, say "trick-or-treat" and get our first pieces of candy.

Trick-or-treating isn't much fun when you live out in the country because there aren't a lot of houses out there. But here, there are houses everywhere, and almost all of them have candy! After just three streets, my bag is already half-filled.

After our fourth street, we turn a corner, and coming right

toward us is a kid dressed as some type of sports player.

Ricky.

"Is that you in there, Lester?" He walks right up to us and knocks on my visor.

Now I know why there's a sign on the fish tank at my dentist's office that says not to tap on the glass. "Stop!" I yell at him. "It's so loud when you do that."

"Okay, okay." He steps back and looks at me for a minute. "So, where'd you get this thing anyway?"

"From his dad," Abby says.

"What is he, like an astronaut or something?" Ricky asks.

"Yeah," I tell him.

"Cool," Ricky says finally. Then he just stands there for a long time looking around and not saying anything.

"Ricky," Abby says, "what are you doing here?"

"Getting candy."

"No. What are you doing here with *us*?"

"Nothing. I'm not doing anything. I just wanted to tell Lester . . ." He stops talking and just stares at me.

"What, Ricky? What do you want to tell me?"

"There's this house around the corner." He points down the street. "A big white house. And they're giving out full-size candy bars." He looks at me for a couple of seconds, knocks on my helmet again even though I told him not to, then runs on down the street. Right before he rounds the corner, he turns back to me. "See you later . . . Space Boy."

It's true. I am a space boy. My dad was an astronaut. I'm wearing a space helmet. I love space more than anything else in the world.

And now it's part of my name.

"I guess you got another nickname," Abby says.

"It's so perfect."

"Perfect? Lester, you hate nicknames."

"Not this one." Then I think of something that makes me smile even bigger. "Do you think everyone's going to start calling me that?"

"Well, I'm not."

"Why?"

"Because you're Lester. I like your name."

"Oh, come on, Abby! Call me Space Boy."

"No."

"Please."

"No." She stomps off toward the next house, then flips around and smiles that big Abby smile of hers. "Well, come on, *Space Boy*. Let's go get our full-size candy bars."

For the next three streets, every time Abby says something to me, she calls me Space Boy, and it sounds better and better each time I hear it.

When our bags are mostly filled and people start turning out their porch lights, it's time to go home. But I don't even mind. For the first time in a long time, everything feels right. Being here with Abby. My new nickname that Ricky gave me. Everything.

Even the sky feels right.

"See that constellation up there, Abby? The one that looks like a stretched-out *W*?" I point up into the sky to show her Cassiopeia, and that's when I see it.

There. Right above our heads. A superstar shoots across the sky.

Abby doesn't say anything. She just reaches over and grabs my hand.

I look over at her, just long enough to see that she's not looking back at me. She's keeping her eyes on the sky. Just like she's supposed to.

Acknowledgments

Much of the time, writing can feel like a solitary activity—a writer alone with her words. But writing is really a process of creation and sharing, of feedback and revision, of self-doubt and loving support. I did not weather any step of this journey alone, and for that, I'm so thankful.

To my former students and colleagues at Lantern Road Elementary School in Fishers, Indiana. You were my very first readers when I started writing *Superstar* so many years ago. You gave me your honest feedback and supported me through my transition from teacher to writing student.

To my faculty advisors at Hamline University's MFA in Writing for Children program—Jane Resh Thomas, Claire

Rudolf Murphy, Kelly Easton, and Anne Ursu. You took my words into your caring hands and challenged me to see my writing in new ways. You believed in me before I started believing in myself.

To my readers and writing buddies—Jennifer Mazi Huffman, Jamie Kallio, Naomi Kinsman, and Peter Pearson. You all have read this book more times than I can remember, each time giving me the feedback I needed to keep going. I couldn't ask for better writing friends.

To my agent, Jennifer Laughran. Your wisdom and extensive knowledge of the publishing world helped guide me through this process. I feel so lucky to have you as my agent.

To everyone at HarperCollins who worked so hard on *Superstar*, especially my editor and friend, Jill Davis. Your insight and critical eye helped make this book what it is today. And if you hadn't encouraged me (so many times) to just finish the darn thing and submit it, Lester might still be hidden away in some folder on my computer.

To my family—Jean Layton, Jack Davis, Rob Davis, Bella Davis, and most of all, my mom, Debby Davis. Your love of the written word is what inspired me to start writing in the first place (when I was five). And even now, you've read every draft of *Superstar* and shared in every step of the process with me. I'm so grateful for all your wisdom, and love.

To my partner, Tony Mulhern. When it comes to you,

thankful doesn't even begin to describe what I feel. You have supported me through draft after draft, through all the joy and all the fear and everything in between. This book would not be what it is without you. And neither would I.